HOW I MADE
MY FIRST
MI££ION

HOW I MADE MY FIRST
MI££ION

SIXTEEN TRUE STORIES
OF HOW BRITISH TYCOONS
MADE THEIR FORTUNES

TAMMY COHEN

metro

Published by John Blake Publishing Ltd,
3 Bramber Court, 2 Bramber Road,
London W14 9PB, England

www.johnblakepublishing.co.uk

First published in hardback in 2009

ISBN: 978 1 84454 686 2

British Library Cataloguing-in-Publication Data:

A catalogue record for this book is available from the British Library.

Design by www.envydesign.co.uk

Printed in the UK by CPI William Clowes Beccles NR34 7TL

1 3 5 7 9 10 8 6 4 2

Papers used by John Blake Publishing are natural, recyclable products
made from wood grown in sustainable forests. The manufacturing processes
conform to the environmental regulations of the country of origin.

For Rikki, who believes all things are possible

ACKNOWLEDGEMENTS

I'd like to thank everyone who helped in the writing of this book, particularly the millionaires who gave so generously of their time and advice, and who opened up about their lives, their dreams and their struggles, so honestly and often so movingly. I'd also like to thank my friends and journalist colleagues as well as the hundreds of press officers and PR personnel who collectively put forward such a diverse and eclectic mix of potential interviewees. It's a shame there wasn't room to follow up each and every one of those suggestions. I'm also indebted also to the PAs of many of the millionaires, who spent a lot of time setting up meetings, responding to queries and generally treading the delicate middle ground between subject and interviewer with tact and forbearance. Finally, I'd like to thank John Wordsworth at John Blake Publishing for his endless patience, Wensley Clarkson for his sound advice and Rikki Waller for providing the room with a view where this book was mostly written.

CONTENTS

INTRODUCTION

The very rich are different from you and me. So says Nick Carraway in F Scott Fitzgerald's *The Great Gatsby*. Well, the self-made rich are even more different, and not just because they have more money.

The self-made rich have something else as well, an extra magic ingredient. Some social commentators insist it's just a question of having the right opportunities and surrounding oneself with the right sort of people. They argue that high achievers like Bill Gates might not have succeeded if they weren't exposed early in life to the environment in which they would later excel. In other words, it's nurture rather than nature that separates the mega-achievers from the rest of us.

Or is it?

'There is nothing difficult or mysterious about success,' says Paul Bassi, MD of Bond Wolfe and number 38 on the *Birmingham Post*'s 2009 list of 50 Richest Midlanders. 'All successful people I know are exactly the same as everyone else – they argue with their kids over homework, they have two arms and two legs. The only difference between them and the next guy is that they think bigger.'

They think bigger and, according to a growing body of opinion they think, well, *differently*. Many people, in particular those interested in analysing the science of wealth creation, insist there's something more than luck or opportunity at work. There's something within the self-made rich, some quality or drive that make them succeed where countless others don't. There exists, say a number of these analysts, such a thing as a Millionaire's Mindset.

In researching this book I have talked to people who became rich overnight and to people who slogged their way to the top. I've talked to people who became rich from their bedrooms, people who became rich because they had something to prove and people who became rich almost by default. Some of the interviewees had accrued money gradually and steadily, others had made and lost vast fortunes, often more than once in their lives, in a violently zig-zagging graph of personal wealth. This was a group of wildly diverse individuals who differed in almost every respect except two – 1) they'd all made lots of money and 2) they shared certain core beliefs.

It's within those shared beliefs that the key to unlocking the secrets of the self-made rich can perhaps be found. Because if it was all about opportunity and luck, wouldn't all people who'd had early access to computers become Bill

Gates? Wouldn't all kids growing up immersed in music turn into the Beatles? What is it that makes some people able to take advantage of opportunities when they come their way? How do some people manage to turn luck into cash? Just what are the guiding principles of the millionaire mindset?

Top of the list must be a willingness to see possibilities. The millionaires I spoke to were not 'yes but...' people, ready at a moment's notice to list ten reasons why an idea wouldn't work. They were, without exception, open to new concepts, new ideas, new ways forward. 'I believe in possibilities rather than barriers,' says DP Connect MD, Toni Cocozza, who started up her own recruitment company without even a chair to sit on.

We all know people who will shoot an idea down in flames before it's even out of your mouth, listing all the things that can go wrong and dismissing it almost before they've had time to take it in properly. Seeing the possibilities means changing that mindset so that you become receptive to what's around you, and able to recognise potential. 'I see things that other people don't see,' says Dominic McVey, who made his first fortune at 15 by importing scooters into the UK. 'That's what I'm good at – looking at what's around me until an idea comes to me.'

Finance guru Stefan Wissenbach insists that the ability to recognise possibilities is sometimes dismissed by other people as luck. 'Luck is what happens when preparation meets opportunity. I'm well attuned to possibilities and when they come along, I recognise them and seize them, while others might just let them pass by.'

But it's not just a question of recognising possibility – the second core belief shared by the millionaires is a willingness to act on that possibility, to take a risk. Most of us are deterred from risk taking not just because of what we have to lose, but also because of the fear of public failure. What will our colleagues say? Our social network? The press? The truth – as any public figure will tell you – is that anyone who makes a splash is going to get noticed and while you risk public disapprobation by failing, you risk it far more by succeeding.

'Sure people will knock you – they always do when you're making a success of something,' observes Kim Einhorn who, together with her brother David, founded the phenomenally successful event organisers Theme Traders. 'Just remember, it doesn't matter.'

But once you've identified an opportunity and psyched yourself up to take the risk, now what? At this stage many of us would get bogged down in cash flow projections, business plans, market research… until we've all but buried our initial plan and enthusiasm under a mountain of paperwork and meaningless jargon. The millionaires, on the other hand, just do it. 'My advice to anyone just starting out is always just go out there and start,' says Toni Cocozza, who admits she'd never have got her company off the ground if she'd had to fill in all the forms and spreadsheets the bank required in order to secure a loan.

Andrew Reynolds, who has made a fortune from his Cash on Demand system of wealth creation, tells the story of two men who finished one of his training courses and went in totally opposite directions. One spent the next month drawing up spreadsheets and grand, detailed four-year projections; the other took out a small ad in his local paper and built up sales from there, one by one. The second man has made over £10million, the first never even got started. 'He couldn't shake off the corporate mentality,' says Reynolds. 'He was too bogged down in forecasting and planning. Perhaps it was his way of hiding from the real truth – that he needed to actually take action.'

Entrepreneur William Berry, who has started up more than his fair share of companies over the course of the last ten years, sums it up like this: 'If you want to do something, don't think too long and hard about it – just go out there and do it. There's no point in talking endlessly about it, or it just won't get done.'

Once you've got your great idea off the ground, there are several key elements to making a success of it. The first, very unglamorously, is hard work. Even a millionaire mindset won't stop you having to get your hands dirty. Kim Einhorn, whose ethos has always been to say 'yes' first and worry afterwards, remembers having to construct an entire mock-up fairground in her own garden, hand-painting each item on her kitchen table and, for another event, hand-stitching 20 pairs of chaps. 'We did everything. I'd drive to Birmingham to do a make-up job that would pay just £75, and David would drive for two hours to entertain at a Harvester. We just accepted every booking that came our way. We worked so hard so that we were never in a position of being unable to pay our mortgage.'

Similarly Dame Mary Perkins, Specsavers MD, recalls working five days a week, plus three evenings and Sunday mornings – all combined with bringing up three small children. 'Looking back, we worked incredibly hard, but at the time it was just how things were. My father had always taught me that I'd have to work for a living and that no one would ever hand me anything on a plate, so I knew financial security wasn't going to fall from a tree and land in my lap. It would be a question of grafting for it.'

Hilary Devey, a single mother, recalls regularly driving through the night while she was trying to get her pallet distribution business off the ground, so she could be there to get her son up in the morning.

But the world is full of grafters. If hard work alone was enough to make fortunes, wouldn't we all be millionaires? Certainly, there are other ingredients in the mix that separate the worker bees from the queen bees, and chief among these is self-belief. It's not that all the interviewees in these pages are puffed up with their own importance. Far from it. While some could be construed as justifiably arrogant, others are quietly confident. Then there are those – such as Toni Cocozza and Pure Package founder Jenny Irvine – who confess to having suffered from low self-esteem. But one thing they all share is the complete conviction that they're good at what they do. 'I've always known I'd succeed again,' says Ben Way, who had made and lost a fortune by the time he was 21. 'It's just been a question of when, rather than if. That might sound arrogant but self-belief is all I know.'

The truth is that if you don't believe you can do something, you haven't got a hope of convincing others. 'You've got to believe in yourself. You've got to have confidence,' insists Nigel Goldman, a trader who made £14million in one day and lost the lot. 'Otherwise you have nothing.'

Once you believe in yourself, you're more likely to give yourself permission to become rich. Think that sounds weird? Not really, because that's another key feature of the self-made rich – they've beaten the 'I'm not worthy' syndrome that most of us, particularly in Britain, are so badly afflicted by. Instead they believe they deserve to make money because, in the words of L'Oreal's famous ad campaign, they're worth it.

But when it comes to making money, belief isn't worth anything unless there's substance behind it. You have to have faith in yourself but, and it's a big but, that faith has to be justified. 'Be honest with yourself,' advises Brad Rosser, once Richard Branson's right-hand man. 'Successful entrepreneurs don't sugar-coat anything.'

Jaeger boss, Harold Tillman, has learned enough over his 50-year career in the fashion industry to realise that being realistic with yourself about your good qualities and about your limitations can save a lot of problems in the long term. 'If I had to give advice to anyone just starting out, I'd say you have to be realistic about your strengths. Flair is something you've either got or you haven't. You can't grow flair.'

Along with self-belief (provided it's not misplaced) building a successful business also requires patience. True, a couple of the millionaires in this book made millions almost overnight, but they lost it again just as quickly. Most have learned the hard way that a business, like a house plant, needs careful nurturing if it's to grow.

Toni Mascolo OBE, MD of hugely successful hairdressers TONI&GUY, credits his childhood obsession with building things for his own success in developing a still-growing empire of salons and product brands. No prizes for guessing that his childhood hero was Julius Caesar. 'He was a strategist and a planner and he was the master empire-builder. Now that I've built a company from nothing I understand how important strategy is if you want to carry on expanding.'

Specsavers is another brand that has grown and evolved from a few stores to a global enterprise with 600 outlets in this country alone. Co-founder Dame Mary Perkins admits that even now, rather than sitting back on her laurels, she's 'constantly looking for ways to expand'.

But even the best-laid plans can – and do – go wrong. It's what happens when the chips are down that shows the true mettle of the millionaire mindset. All the millionaires I interviewed had come up against obstacles. Many of them had gone bust, some more than once. All had taken knocks and set-backs, but not one had given up. 'I've made a lot of mistakes,' says transport tycoon, Hilary Devey, 'but I needed to make them. I learned from them.'

Ben Way, who read he was next to Robbie Williams on the *Sunday Times* Rich List on the same day he couldn't afford to buy a tube ticket, knows more than most just how hard failure can be, coming hot on the heels of success. 'When you're 19 years old and have got used to being told you're the best thing since sliced bread, you fall hard,' he says. What's essential is that you jump back up again. 'Don't be afraid of failure,' he says. 'My failure has definitely made me a better person.'

Stefan Wissenbach points out that Britain has a very different attitude towards failure than America. 'In the States, if you haven't failed, you haven't risked and, more importantly, you haven't learned. In the UK if you've failed you're a failure.'

Don't forget that failure can also be used to your advantage. For Toni Mascolo, the rare failure of a business venture in Italy opened the door for other opportunities to expand the company in America instead. 'So though at the time this was our biggest disaster, it was also the start of our biggest opportunity. Because you never know, do you? When you think, God, this is the greatest disaster of my life, it could also be the greatest opportunity of your life.'

But while failure can be a stepping-stone to bigger and

better things, that only happens when you learn from your mistakes. In that respect all the millionaires were united. 'You start to think, Can I recover from this?' says Harold Tillman, recalling the collapse of Honorbilt, the men's clothing company he was running. 'But you can't afford to think like that for long.'

Even when things are running smoothly, there are still inherent dangers in running a business. The number one danger is complacency. Businesses have to be organic: they have to keep evolving and changing in order to stay with the marketplace. The interviewees in this book were all forward thinkers, all thinking ahead to the next opportunity for growth, the next big idea.

'We want to inhabit the space others aren't in – to get there before everyone else, and leave just as they all arrive,' says Paul Bassi, whose company, Bond Wolfe, has made a fortune 'reading' the markets.

What's the best way to make sure you keep moving forward? Goal-setting. Several of the interviewees in the book cited the example of study that was done on Yale graduates. Of the Class of 1953, only three per cent were found to have formulated and written down their goals for the future. When the researchers returned to the group 20 years later, that three per cent was worth more, in financial terms, than the other 97 per cent combined. Little wonder then that the men and women featured in this book write a lot of lists. Brad Rosser, king of the start-up businesses, remembers that when he worked with Richard Branson, the Virgin boss was rarely seen without a little notebook in his hand on which he recorded his daily 'to do' list.

Here's Paul Bassi again: 'I have daily goals, weekly goals annual goals, five-yearly goals and what I call Big Picture Goals. I've recorded and kept every goal I ever set myself – everything from buying a new suit to buying a car or a property, getting my children educated, or travel and fitness.'

Andrew Reynolds recalls that back in 1997, when he was stuck in a soul-destroying salaried job he hated, he wrote out a list of five-year goals:

- A house worth at least £500,000 paid for in cash
- At least £500,000 in cash, in the bank
- A top of the range BMW
- A housekeeper
- A gardener

He kept that list of goals by his bed and recited it every night. By 2002, every single one of them had come true.

Entrepreneur and dating site boss, Ross Williams, goes even further and advocates making your goals public. 'True some people might take the mickey or secretly want you to fail, but it gives you the best incentive to succeed.'

So what happens, you might ask, when all the goals are reached? After all, you can only live in one massive house, only drive one flashy car. What happens to these obsessive goal-setters when all the goals are reached? The answer is that they set a different type of goal. The individuals I spoke to for this book are still getting up in the morning, still coming into work, still making deals, long after the material need to do so has passed, but today their motivation is different. For many of them, the urge to create wealth is now more directed at other people than for themselves. They want to create a secure base for their families, or for the greater good. By making sure their companies keep evolving and making money, they're able to contribute to a range of causes far removed from the business world.

Sometimes the motivation to keep going is just because they don't know any other way. Put simply, many of the interviewees in this book have got the Making Money Gene. Look at Jenny Irvine, who started up a business selling eggs from her parents' farm to restaurants at just eight years old. Or Dominic McVey who, at less than ten years of age, stole his father's credit card and started buying shares online. Nigel Goldman made tens of thousands trading in rare coins while still at school. Ben Way was courted by venture capitalists when he was just 16. It's in the blood in a way that spending days sitting around a spa or hitting balls around a golf course is not. 'What else would I do?' exclaims Dame Mary Perkins. 'Sit at home and knit?'

So, self-made successful people are open to possibility – they're risk-takers, they're persistent, they're resilient. They set goals, they think ahead and see the bigger picture, and when they fall down (which they often do) they get right back up again. And when they get to where they were aiming to go, they don't retire to their yachts. They just re-set the finishing line and, in Toni Mascolo's phrase 'start a new race'.

There's no exam you can take to become a millionaire, no magic formula, no tried and tested route. You can't set your GPS for success and assume it'll guide you there. But maybe by reading the honest, often moving, always fascinating accounts in this book, you'll get some insight into how other people have done it – a glimpse inside the so-called millionaire's mindset. And as the accounts are all in the first person with the individuals' voices coming through loud and strong, you'll come away with a sense of how diverse this group of people is, yet how much common ground they share. In the end, business is all about people – and people come in all shapes and sizes, all colours and fittings. There's no template for success, but perhaps, if you read carefully, there's a guide.

The people in this book have, as the 'nurture over nature' advocates point out, had fortunate opportunities and surrounded themselves with good support systems, but they've also strategised, slogged, bluffed, envisioned, battled and sometimes just chutzpah'd their way to success. They've had the same dreams as you or I, but they've dreamed that bit bigger, set the bar that bit higher.

If they can do it, isn't there just a chance that we could do it too?

CHAPTER 1

ANDREW REYNOLDS
LESSONS LEARNED

*Judging by his father and his grandfathers, 51-year-old
entrepreneur Andrew Reynolds believes he was
genetically predisposed to fail in business. So how did he
break the hereditary mould and make £30m working
from his own home?*

The other Friday morning, I stood in the hallway of a beautifully furnished, three-bedroom house in the centre of an historic Kent town with my arms around my mum as she sobbed with joy. This was the woman who, together with my dad, had sacrificed so much to bring me up, who'd gone without new clothes, without food sometimes, struggling to raise a family. Now I'd been able to do what I'd always sworn I'd do even as a very young boy – buy my mum her own home. It's moments like that which remind me why I've made the choices I have in my life, and just how far I've come.

When I was born, my parents were hard up and struggling for money – something that, sadly, was to remain constant throughout their lives together. We lived in a one-bedroom caravan on a site outside Winchester. My dad had made a paltry living as a door-to-door insurance salesman before moving on to a paraffin delivery round that he

3

bought from a guy for £50. His new business involved driving door to door in a van towing a trailer. (For those not old enough to remember, paraffin heaters were the most popular form of household heating before central heating really came in. Each week the paraffin guy would come around and deliver maybe five gallons of the fuel, which you then put in your heaters.) He'd had grandiose ideas of being his own boss but like most similar businessmen Dad had actually bought himself a manual labour job. But he was happy – he had his name on the side of his van and he was 'in business'.

With the imminent arrival of my baby brother a few years after me, my parents somehow managed to wangle a mortgage to get a house and we moved into a modest terraced 'two up, two down' with an outside toilet. After the caravan it felt almost palatial. But Dad quickly discovered that the heating business is rather seasonal, and inevitably the paraffin round failed to yield the financial returns he had been dreaming of. So he sought other ways to make money.

When I was about 10 or 11, we moved into a different house, adjoining a shop in the town that Dad had rented for a new business he was starting. It was to be a hardware and DIY store and, as with all his business ventures, Dad was convinced it would be a sure-fire success and bring him the financial security he craved.

Having no capital, everything was bought on credit. The fact that he struggled almost from day one and that both the house and the shop were crying out for essential maintenance work, didn't stop him from persuading the owners to sell him the freeholds a few years after we moved in. That was a financial disaster. Trying to scrape together the mortgage payment on both properties month in, month out, while the queues of eager customers he'd envisaged failed to materialise, meant there was no money left over for repairs. I can still see the pained look on his face every time it rained as he ran around the shop putting buckets and containers under all the holes in the roof to stop the stock getting damaged by the rainwater. It was no better in the house. A hole in the roof in one corner meant that water would pour down the walls when it rained and eventually the plasterwork fell away leaving a hole and a damp, musty smell that pervaded every room.

From the age of 11 I worked in the shop on Saturdays and during school holidays, to help the family business – serving customers all day to bring the money in. But despite the whole family working in the shop – which was open six days a week – the business never made any real money. It bounced along the line of solvency – just about providing enough money for food and clothing for the family. But Dad was happy because he had his name over the door.

Despite the material hardship I must say that I had a very happy childhood. Occasionally I would feel the effects of not having money – mainly at Christmas time when my friends at school would turn up with new bikes or wearing nice new clothes, but otherwise it didn't really register with me. I accepted it as normal. The only time I remember being consciously unhappy with what we had was when Dad took me to Heathrow Airport for a rare day out. We went up on an observation deck and I recall him saying, 'Look at that one – I wonder where they are off to?' I remember thinking, I don't want to stand here watching other people fly off – I want to be on the damn plane!

I always had this gut feeling that someone somewhere knew a different way to make money than the struggle I witnessed my Dad go through day in day out.

I didn't do particularly well at school. I have a low boredom threshold and I never took lessons very seriously. I find it almost impossible to learn from reading a book. I scraped through, ending up with just four O levels (one of which was woodwork and another was technical drawing) – proving you don't need to be a genius to be successful in business!

I never had that competitive gene to do well at school that some people have. I think there is a perception that 'successful' business people were big successes throughout life – the best at sports, the best at attracting the opposite sex, the best at school – but it isn't necessarily that way. Take sports for example. I was always the guy who got picked last to be on a team by the other players. I was useless! Give me a bat and a ball and I'll show you a very strong lack of hand/eye coordination.

To be honest, school was more or less a non-event in my life. I think the teachers just saw me as an average student – nothing special with no special skills, a guy who would merge into the background and never really be anything outstanding in life. I didn't have that urge to excel, even at college. I was just an ordinary, middle of the road bloke. Most of my attitude was formed by my family and what went on at home.

I never felt particularly stigmatised at school through not having much money. I went to the local secondary modern (I'd fallen just short of the required exam results to make grammar school) so everyone was more or less in the same boat. But even at school I was quite good at making money. I remember there was a craze for water pistols when I was about 11. Everyone wanted them. (Everyone needed one to defend themselves!) I found a newsagents shop where you could buy them for half the price the kids were paying locally. Having no cash myself, I took orders with full payment up front, then went to my 'supplier' and bought his stock. I guess that must have made an impression, as my businesses today all revolve around positive cash flow. Customers send me money – then we send the goods. We don't give credit!

I also talked my form tutor into letting us start a breakfast-time tuck shop in an old stationary cupboard. We served assorted drinks to other kids for a small profit, all of which we gave to a campaign to raise money for a school minibus.

One of the few things I enjoyed about school was putting on shows. That's probably why I get so much pleasure now out of running my seminar and conference business. It's great to find something you love doing and then figure out a way to make money from it.

When I was coming up to 16, I recall the careers advisor

visiting the school and being most surprised that I had no idea what I wanted to 'be' when I left school. I stared at my feet, trying to think of anything to say to break the silence, and when no inspiration came to me I mumbled something about going into business. Before I knew what had happened, she'd pigeonholed me for the Business Diploma course at the local technical college. Another box ticked for her.

And so I went on to do a Diploma in Business Studies – the biggest waste of two years in my life! I scraped through that, although I failed accountancy. I believe I had the distinction of being the only student ever to fail that subject. My accounts tutor was beside himself, particularly as he set the questions and had coached me in exactly the sort of questions likely to come up! Needless to say there were grave concerns that someone who could not achieve even a modest 45 per cent pass in accountancy could ever do well in business.

After scraping through college I went from job to job, working in a camera shop, as a trainee estate agent, toy shop assistant, then a travelling sales rep selling toys and dolls. It was all pretty aimless until eventually I found something I was quite good at – selling houses on new homes sites. For some reason I did very well at this and gradually climbed the corporate ladder, ending up on the main board of one of the country's larger house-builders – a job I absolutely detested.

I had a big salary and lots of perks, but the day-to day

grind of doing something that didn't fulfil me just to make someone else rich took its toll. I became increasingly unhappy and my marriage foundered under the strain of my huge disappointment with my life. The situation reached a peak in 1997 on my 40th birthday when, probably like a lot of people, I started to question what the hell I was doing with my life and I began to look for alternatives.

A few years earlier I'd bought some motivational videos, in which an American guy explained how to make thousands of dollars a month working from home. I'd almost forgotten about these videos, but when I got a computer at work and started surfing the net, I discovered this guy had a website. I emailed him on impulse and he emailed me back an invitation to attend a seminar in the US. There are some moments that really do change your life. The moment I made the decision to take a week off work and attend this seminar in Las Vegas was definitely one of them.

All the way there I was wondering what on earth I was doing, but the main speaker – a shy, reclusive sort of guy – struck a chord with his talk: How to Make $30,000 a Month Working from Home. This was a guy who was not talking theory – he was actually doing what he was teaching – and it made so much sense to me. He talked at length about low overheads, low cost/high margin products, the lifetime value of a customer and how to build a million-pound business from home. I remember he stood on stage, held up a CD and explained: 'My customer sends me money – in this case $897. I run off a copy of the CD

– a blank CD costs me less than a dollar – and I ship it to him. I make around $890 profit on every order I get. My business model is to get four or five orders a day.'

That was it for me. By the time I flew back from the US, something inside me had shifted. Completely recklessly, I went into my boss's office and handed in my notice. He was astounded. He honestly could not understand how I could be unhappy in my job or why I hated every single minute of each working day. The wave of relief I felt on resigning was quickly overshadowed by the thought, Oh God, what have I done now? I'd given up a good salary, company car, decent career, all on the basis of something I had learned in the US and reckoned I would like to try in the UK. Colleagues and friends thought I was mad. I had a prime corporate job – the kind most people dream of. I also had an ex-wife to support and other financial obligations. But deep down I just *knew* this was the thing that was going to change my life.

I had to work a one-year notice period – which meant I could get my business up and running only in my spare time at weekends and in the evenings. Some nights I would go to bed just a couple of hours before I had to get up for the day job. It was extremely gruelling, but worth it. Six months into my notice period the company was bought out by another builder, who thankfully did not impose the rest of my contract and allowed me leave six months early. I was free.

I still had moments of blind panic. A few years earlier, during the last big recession, I'd been out of work and I remembered vividly running out of money and surviving on a box of Rice Krispies for a whole week. I was absolutely determined never to go back to that again. Certainly there were a few nights when I sat up late with a large drink, thinking, Oh my God, you just threw away a safe corporate salary and you have no idea if this will work or not.

But the business side of things was pretty straightforward. When I was in the US, I'd spoken to the seminar company and agreed to purchase a UK licence for a set of videos of a seminar on Internet Marketing they'd held a few months earlier. This was a relatively new topic in the US and certainly new to the UK, which was only slowly getting online with dial-up connections. The deal was that in return for a modest licence fee, I could sell as many copies as I wanted in the UK and keep all the profits. The value of the information on the tapes for people aspiring to learn about the internet and how to make money using it was huge. Like Dad, who'd opened up a DIY shop despite being pretty clueless about fixing things around the house, I had no idea how this internet stuff worked. But I reckoned I could market the tapes as a publisher, working from my spare room at home. Which is exactly what I did.

Of course there were plenty of doubters – people fully prepared to give me the benefit of their advice and tell me why I didn't have a hope of succeeding. When I'd returned from the US that first time, full of enthusiasm and clutching video footage of what I had seen, I got a less than enthusiastic response when I showed it to a few people. My dad said it simply would not work. I tried to explain to colleagues at work what I was going to be doing and they all tried to talk me out of it. The problem? None of them could make a reasoned judgement based on experience because what they were looking at was outside of their realm of knowledge. I learned a valuable lesson from that period – always ignore outside advice!

The business quickly grew from strength to strength as I reinvested the profits in more licences from my contact in the US. I had ten video recorders all plugged together in the cupboard under the stairs in my little house. When I got orders, I would get blank tapes from Makro or Currys, run off copies and ship them to my customer. When you consider that the blank tapes cost me less than £1 and I could sell a set of 20 for around £697, it was easy to make money – even for a guy who doesn't understand accounts!

I then decided to take it one step further by holding my own seminars on making money from home, inviting the US speakers to come over to speak in London and filming the event myself. Even today the businesses I still run follow the same basic model. We hold seminars and workshops at which we feature speakers from around the world. These events are filmed – making another saleable product on DVD. From that one simple business model we have so far generated over £30milliom in sales – not bad for a business that started out of my back bedroom.

With the benefit of hindsight, I can see that witnessing my dad's struggles in business while I was growing up, helped me not repeat those mistakes when I started up on my own. From Dad's experience, I learned some valuable, hard-won lessons:

- The business model of a small retail shop is fundamentally flawed. Taking out a bank loan to buy goods from a wholesaler so there is stock on the shelves, in the hope that someone will want them, is not a recipe for success. This is particularly true when the shop is in a secondary location in town. Today, the business model I use has almost no stock and no retail premises. In fact, most of the business can be run on autopilot through a fulfilment house and can therefore be run at arm's length from almost anywhere in the world via my laptop.

- My dad's shop used to hold around 16,000 items of stock – a huge amount of inventory to store. My business sells DVDs, CDs and printed materials – all of which can be produced almost on demand, doing away with the need for large piles of stock.

- A retail shop is a service business too. As a small shopkeeper, what Dad was really selling was his time. He would sit behind the counter in the shop from 9am to 6pm waiting for people to wander by, call in and make a purchase. He prided himself on serving people personally and he could spend half an hour of his day with someone, just to sell them a few packets of nails or some shelving brackets. When I started my business, I was determined that it would provide a different lifestyle from the one Dad had. I didn't want to spend 25 years of my life staring out of a shop window waiting for someone to walk in and buy. The business I now run uses direct response marketing techniques to market its products. When I want to sell some products I go out to the market and make a noise. When the money is in, I move on to the next project. Most of this is handled for me by outsourced companies, which means I can work when I want and where I want. As long as I have access to an internet connection I can do business.

- My dad was the first to admit he was not a practical sort of person. His DIY skills were non-existent. Even the simplest of repair jobs would go wrong for him. Yet he decided to open a DIY store where he was asked for advice by all his customers, who saw him as the expert because his name was above the door. You don't have to be an expert in your chosen business − as long as you don't put yourself in a position where you're being asked for advice. When I started, for example, I was not selling my expertise. I became the publisher of other people's expertise and quickly made money without people asking me for my opinion.

- Dad's friends were mainly people from the same background − small shopkeepers and one-man bands like himself. In fact his only source of business advice − apart from these friends − were his bank manager and his accountant. These were two people he looked up to and sought advice from about his business, although they'd never actually run one themselves. I learned never to take advice from your accountant or your bank manager. What do they know? The accountant knows how to keep the score and the bank manager knows how to find ways to make money from money. Neither would do well if you set them adrift and told them to start a business. They have no practical business experience. Why ask their advice? More importantly, why take it?

- I also never take advice from failed business people. When I run one of my workshops, to teach people about starting and running a home-based business, I normally find that the loudest voice in the room – the guy who wants to share his opinion and experience on every single topic – is the guy who has failed completely at business. Be careful about who you take advice from. When I took the college course after leaving school, I found that most of the people teaching me 'business' were not successful business people. They were professional teachers with little or no business experience. Years later, when I started my business, I found someone who had done exactly what I wanted to do – and I learned directly from him.

Those were the lessons I learned from dear old hard-working Dad, who'd slogged all his life but never managed to achieve financial stability. In contrast to his experience, I knew very early on that my business was going to be a big success. In 1997, a few months before I received the invitation to attend the seminar in the US, I'd read a book that was based around the law of attraction. (This was way before anyone had heard of a film called *The Secret*) and I had written a five-year 'vision' on a piece of paper. It said:

By 20 October 2002 I will have:
- A house worth at least £500,000 paid for in cash
- At least £500,000 in cash in the bank
- A top of the range BMW
- A housekeeper
- A gardener

I kept that piece of paper in my bedside drawer and for five years I recited that list over and over each night. It was a completely impossible list when I first wrote it – there was no way I could afford it on the salary I was on. But on 2 September 2002 I moved into my £1million house, which I had just paid for in cash. I had more than £500,000 in the bank. I had a BMW 7 Series on the drive and someone to clean my house and someone to tend the garden. Every single thing on my list came true!

Yet I'm not most people's stereotype of a successful businessman. I would describe myself as a very shy person, which is weird for a guy who gets up on stage and speaks to 4,000-plus people! And I am far from confident. This can sometimes work against me. I hate, for example, networking events – the business breakfast is something that fills me with horror. With every new project I launch, I'm always jittery, wondering if this will be the one that doesn't work. Oddly, before a launch, I will wake in the middle of the night sweating from a nightmare of being back in corporate life with my boss breathing down my neck. But I never take anything for granted. I check and ponder over every little detail of a project.

If you looked at my inheritance, you'd probably say I'm genetically destined to fail. My paternal grandfather ran a series of small businesses and never made a lot of money, ending his days on state benefits. My maternal grandfather – a lovely guy – ran his own small building company as well as being preacher at his local church. His business ended up going bust, although he made sure that every single creditor got paid fully, such was his integrity as a man. My own father failed in business and passed away in poverty. It could be argued that I am therefore likely to fail too, but in my view, success in business is not about being born with that special something. Business is something that can be learned – as long as you learn from someone who has done it, rather than a teacher offering theories and who has never done it for himself.

I get so many people coming to me saying, 'I've developed this great product – now who can I sell it to? Would you help me sell it?' In my view, that's completely the wrong way round. I learned very quickly that the way to stack the deck in your favour in business is first to identify a small crowd of hungry people. Then it's a question of finding something which will satisfy their hunger – and standing in the middle collecting the cash.

So many people also spend loads of time doing all of the start-up nonsense. They buy all the business administration books, the starter set of stationery with matching envelopes from the print shop, and are particularly proud when they see their name on their own business cards and compliment slips. They also have meetings with the small business advisor at their local bank. This wet-behind-the-ears advisor has never owned a business himself and is not qualified to provide business advice – he is trained to seek out opportunities for sales of insurances, pensions and other profit-generating bank products. So these aspiring entrepreneurs have spent some money, busied themselves and taken advice, yet they still have no business. I'd rather get some cash coming in first, then worry about the admin stuff later.

At one of my training workshops, I once taught two guys how to copy my business model and get started themselves. One guy came back a month later with a huge range of spreadsheets, a 'critical path analysis' and a complete four-year projection, showing line by line the likely profit and loss of his theoretical new business. The other guy called me a month later and said, 'I just placed my first tiny ad in the paper and my first sales came in.' The second guy has now pulled in around £10million using what I taught him. The other guy never got off the starting blocks. He couldn't shake off the corporate mentality: he was too bogged down in forecasting and planning. Perhaps it was his way of hiding from the real truth – that he needed to actually take action.

Nowadays I still stick to the core business model we've always had, but I've also diversified a little. Whatever business I start up, I always try to keep it lean so we can adjust to changes in markets. For example, I launched a TV shopping channel not long ago (The Entrepreneur Channel plc – Sky 682). It has been successful and very unusually for a new business, it made money in its first year of broadcasting – something almost unheard of in the industry.

We achieved this by using solid direct-response marketing techniques that I have used so successfully in my other businesses, by having a sound business model and by keeping overheads down to the bare bone. The TV business, for example, consists of just two people – myself and an operations director. Everything else is outsourced. We use freelance camera people, freelance graphics. We use a fulfilment centre to handle the orders and a call centre to take phone calls. Contrast that with other TV companies, which have thousands of staff, huge headquarters buildings and all the other trappings of corporate success.

My success in business has allowed me to do a lot to help other people. A few years ago I came up with the idea of holding an event called the Entrepreneurs Bootcamp. As well as helping wannabe businessmen learn about entrepreneurship, its primary aim was to raise money for good causes. My plan from the outset was that 100 per cent of the ticket proceeds would go directly to charity, with no admin fees or costs to be deducted towards putting on the event. With absolutely no idea whether it would work, I rented Wembley Conference Centre and within three weeks had sold almost every seat – around 2,500 people. We raised over £325,000 from that one event, which we handed to Great Ormond Street children's charity. You can't imagine the feeling of accomplishment when I visited the hospital. To walk in through those doors and see the kids being treated in a brand new room I had raised the money to build was indescribable.

Since then I have organised a couple more such events and raised well over £1million for children's charities. Now I'm planning even larger events. Being in business for myself has been a steep learning curve, and I intend to carry on putting the skills I have been fortunate to learn to good use. For example, I recently funded the Make Your Mark with a Tenner campaign, where we gave ten thousand £10 notes to school kids and gave them a month to make a profit. The scheme was designed to teach them about practical business and social enterprise. The winner made a profit of £410 in just 30 days.

One of my goals is to help provide more business mentoring. I know that if my own father had had a mentor to guide him in the right direction, his life could have been so different. I've seen very real results along these lines, through being a patron of the Prince's Trust, but I want to do even more. I am currently working on plans for a major business training facility, in which real-world business people will pass on their knowledge and experience to others. But that's a few years off yet.

On a personal level, my lifestyle has changed immeasurably since making my first million. Instead of dreading going into work, I now love what I do. My desire on day one was to make myself and my family financially secure. I never had a great desire to grow huge corporations with loads of shareholder meetings, five-year forecasts and all that nonsense. My emphasis was on relaxation, de-stressing and enjoying life.

Nowadays I have a couple of houses in the UK – one of which is right on the beach in a quiet little unspoilt area. I love the solitude, the peace and quiet and the sound of the waves when I wake. I have a housekeeper who looks after the houses for me, takes care of all my domestic stuff and cooks me fabulous meals. That is worth so much more to me than being at the head of some great corporation, taking calls from shareholders. I've built my businesses so they can be run remotely, so I don't go into work: I can work from my home overlooking the sea or, for formal meetings, my office in Surrey. I'm not particularly interested in cars. I have a Bentley Continental GT, which I love, but rather than change it every year for the latest model, I prefer to keep it for a number of years.

So what drives me to keep running businesses? I get a huge sense of accomplishment from coming up with a project idea – working it through, putting the offer out to the market and seeing the results come in. It's more about that than simply making money, though that is still important to me too. It still seems incredible to me that I started a business from my spare room at home and pulled in over £30million in sales in just ten years. But I don't spend a lot of time thinking about numbers. I never really count my net worth – I don't consider myself in a contest. There is always someone with a lot more. But I do get a real kick out of the fact that I have absolutely no debts – I don't use a credit card, I have no mortgage, no car loan, nothing.

A mentor of mine – a wealthy gentleman who I guess is in his mid-eighties – has started and sold loads of businesses and he still 'works' from home, even today. He says it keeps him going! Contrast that with the chairman of one of the house-building companies I worked for. He retired at 65, ready to relax and start enjoying life after the stress of running the business. Within weeks of retiring and taking it easy, he was struck down by a fatal heart attack. You see so many stories of people dying quickly after they retire.

We've all been sold the myth that you work at something you don't particularly like but at 65 you get to retire and all will be rosy. To me that makes no sense. If you love what you do – if you get a buzz out of it, if it makes you glad to get up in the morning –why on earth would you give that up?

CHAPTER 2

PAUL BASSI

THINK BIGGER, RUN FASTER

A childhood spent helping out in his father's corner shop convinced Paul Bassi there had to be more to life. Now 46 and worth a reputed £40million, the West Midlands-based property investor insists he still hasn't reached his finishing post.

When people call me a success it doesn't ring true to me, because no matter how well my company is doing, or how much money I have personally in the bank, I have yet to meet my own targets. If you're running a 200m race, you're not a success if you only get to the 100m mark – no matter how fast you've run. I have set my own private targets and I will not consider myself successful until I have reached my own finishing line or achieve my own big picture.

That uncompromising attitude was forged very early on in my life. I was a quiet child, but when I decided to do something I always had to excel – whether it was football, marbles, running, jumping or whatever. I just didn't give myself another option. I had to be good at everything. If there was a 100m sprint, I had to excel. If it was a game of conkers, I had to excel.

I'm a Sikh Punjabi Indian and my family were first-generation immigrants working in factories and corner shops, so the work ethic was very deeply ingrained in me from a very young age. I didn't see a lot of my father. He was of that generation that didn't see parenting as his responsibility. His job was to hold down three or four different jobs and put food on the table, not nurture his children. That was left to my mother and grandmother, who did a fantastic job under very difficult circumstances.

I was born in Birmingham but my parents moved to Southall in west London when I was six. My father felt the job prospects were better in London and he eventually found work in a frozen food factory. My mother would look after my brother, sister and me, as well as work from home as a sewing machinist paid per item. She would work every hour she could, early in the morning until late at night and we would all help as much as we could, as we knew that every finished garment meant more income for the family. This was desperately needed to feed us, pay the mortgage and look after my grandmother and my father's youngest sister, who lived with us. My father, as the eldest son, had accepted responsibility to marry her off, and even in those days Indian weddings cost a small fortune.

I recall that when I was about seven, my father had an old sky-blue Vauxhall Viva, which was parked some 200 yards away from our house. I asked my mother several times why it was left so far away but she would never answer. It was only later that she told me it had run out of petrol and that they couldn't afford to buy more as they needed the money for food for my brother, sister and me. If I close my eyes I can still see the exact place where that was car parked on Park Avenue, Southall.

After we'd lived in London a year or two, my parents had saved up enough for a small house. This became a pattern. We always had tenants and my parents would refurbish each house, then buy another house and then another. My brother and I, who were only seven and four at the time, were the maintenance team. We'd be dropped off at a property and told to clean up, do the garden etc. It never occurred to us to complain. In fact it felt good to be able to contribute to the family cause.

When I was 11, my parents sold the houses and bought a corner shop and we lived above it. I was expected to be up in the morning, working behind the counter both before and after school, and out and about delivering groceries and doing whatever else needed to be done.

There was only one time I can remember resenting having to work so hard. I was about 18 and by that time my dad owned a fish and chip shop. It was very successful and on this occasion there was a huge queue so, even though I was desperate to go out with my friends, I had to stay behind and assist. I remember the frustration of watching the time ticking away and knowing I was missing out, but apart from that one time I just accepted that work was something you did to help out. This was also where I was working during the Southall race riots in 1980, when I experienced first hand how vile and violent racism can be.

In the 1970s Southall had an influx of immigrants but there weren't enough school places for us, so we used to get sent to schools outside the area, and were bussed out along the A40 to a school in Acton. I was one of only a few children of Asian origin, but while I was at primary school, no one ever treated me any differently, as young children don't see colour and do not discriminate. At secondary school I was good at sports and I think if you excel at things, you're less likely to be bullied. Every now and then someone would say, 'It's OK that you're a Paki, because you're not like the others,' and although I found this comment offensive, I understood it was their way of saying they accepted me.

As I got older, I became more aware of social divisions and the fact that racial abuse existed. But because I was captain of the football team, I was always protected from the worst of the racism, although I did experience it occasionally while playing football. Paradoxically, it would always bring out the best in me.

It was at secondary school that I was told by my history teacher that I would never achieve anything, and I should come to terms with my very limited future prospects. That teacher would find it hard to believe I have since received an Honorary Doctorate from Birmingham City University, been appointed High Sheriff of the West Midlands by Buckingham Palace and been regional chairman of and UK strategy advisor to Coutts bank. Or that I would be the first Asian president of the Chamber of Commerce and the youngest recipient of the Lloyds TSB Lifetime Achievement Award for services to business and the community, not to mention chairman of one of the largest privately owned property services companies in the UK and chief executive of a company quoted on the stock market. I guess it would be nice to meet up with her for a coffee and update her on a few things – not to gloat but to point out that discouraging youngsters is not particularly responsible.

Occasionally now people will ask me if I'm driven to succeed to show the denigrators how well I've done, but that has never entered my thoughts. The biggest pressure has always been put on me by myself – no one else.

As a teenager, I was constantly thinking up ways to make money. When I was ten, my mother bought me a pair of Adidas rip-off football boots for £1.99 from Woolworths. Having used them to score the winning goal in a school final, I sold them two years later for £2.50 and I had done my first deal. I just had that kind of mindset. I was always putting up little posters in the family's corner shop window promoting this or that. I was constantly thinking ahead, of ways to earn money for the family.

Even today, apart from when I'm playing sport, I'm never really in the moment – I'm always thinking about what will happen next. It's a flaw really, as being constantly in the next moment leaves you unable to enjoy the present one. When I got married recently in the world's only seven-star hotel in Dubai, I thought there might be one moment where I allowed myself to rejoice in the here and now, reflecting on how far I'd come. But even then it didn't happen, although I did get immense pleasure from being with and seeing my family and friends enjoy themselves.

I was never pushed academically by my parents. They probably hoped I would take over the family businesses, so education wasn't so important to them. They'd never had much education themselves so they didn't appreciate the value of it. Going to sixth form college was the furthest anyone of my generation in my family had gone with education. I wasn't terribly motivated academically, preferring sport to studies, and I was too busy working to concentrate on homework. In addition to helping out my parents, I worked in a bakery on night shifts (to this day the smell of baking bread turns my stomach) and squeezed in part-time jobs in a hotel and at a Heathrow airport cargo company in the holidays. But I was driven by the thought of getting away from home. I didn't want to spend every evening and every weekend working behind a counter. Going away to polytechnic college was my ticket out.

I got reasonable enough A levels to win a place at college in Birmingham to study business studies. My dad didn't want me to go but my mum persuaded him. My only career goal at that point was to get a white-collar job. At the age of 13, I'd seen an advert for a civil service job that earned £2,500 a year – £50 a week – and that looked pretty good to me. Anything was better than a factory job, working behind the till in a corner shop, or frying fish and chips.

That's also what lay behind my decision to start work as a trainee legal executive, just after finishing A levels, which I left to go to college.

Studying for an HND in business studies and living away from home was a huge social learning and maturing curve. I came from a very disciplined orthodox Sikh family, so living away from home gave me a great sense of freedom. I went to every party and every gathering going. I met people from all over the world, from every culture and this developed my personality. To this day, I enjoy surrounding myself with an eclectic selection of people, regardless of cast, colour, creed, age, sex or religion, or financial and social status. In fact, looking back, college was just one big party. I'd go back home for holidays and spend the days working in the chip shop and being a dutiful son, then term time would start again and I'd be out partying and chasing girls – which was very 'un-Indian' but I knew I was doing no harm. It was like having two separate lives.

The partying obviously didn't help my studies, but I learned quickly that by pooling resources with my fellow students, we'd be able to get by. I am sometimes referred to as a 'master delegator' and that skill came out of my time at college. I worked out who in the class was good at accounts and who was good at marketing. My own strengths lay in strategy, decision-making and pulling things together behind the scenes, and by joining forces with my friends we all graduated. That hammered home to me the value of teamwork and specialising.

Despite being a very quiet person, I always seemed to take the lead in projects. I always stepped up to the plate and took the initiative if something needed to be done. I think being successful at sports helped develop that willingness to assume responsibility.

When I got my HND in July 1983, I had a steady girlfriend and was having too good a time to want to go home to the chip shop. I knew I had to earn some money if I was to be independent and be allowed to stay away from home, as my father would want me to return home and work in one of his fish and chip shops. So I got myself a white-collar job as an investment broker on a commission-only deal. At first it was just a means to an end – a way of staying in Birmingham – but within six months I'd become the best broker in the firm. I set myself a target of earning £1,000 a month. At that stage, in 1983, I knew no one who earned that much a month, but I managed it – and significantly more in some months – and that gave me self-confidence. I had an opportunity to start a career.

From the outset, I was asset-driven and within a year of starting work, I had bought my own house. The price tag was £20,500 and I'd managed to save 10 per cent for a deposit. It was a three-bedroom modern semi in West Bromwich – the newest house I'd ever been in in my life. Letting myself inside for the first time with my own set of keys was a great feeling, but as usual it didn't last long. I wanted to buy more houses!

To go with my new house, I bought myself a brand new

black Ford Escort XR3i. For a while I thought I was pretty cool, but then I went through a bit of a confused period. When I had started work, my goals had been to earn £1,000 a month, buy my own house, drive a new car and go out with gorgeous girls. Within just a year I'd achieved all my goals and it left me floundering. At this stage I had no mentor and knew nobody more successful than me. So I started to read extensively, particularly about high profile successful individuals. I began to develop new goals, and today I have more than ever before. Some are financial, but mostly I want to experience life to the full and fulfil my potential and help others around me fulfil theirs. Watching those around me achieve now gives me more pleasure than almost anything else.

When the directors of the brokerage firm I worked for parted company and the company was divided into two, the head guy from the 'other' firm came to see me and my friend Rory, who also worked with me. He offered us a basic salary of £30,000 per year and a BMW to join his new firm, Bond Wolfe. Of course we were tempted and went to work there, but it didn't take us long to realise that all the things he'd offered us weren't going to materialise. So we confronted the boss and told him that, if he didn't start paying us the offered sum, we would have no choice but to leave, and all the staff would follow us.

'Why don't you buy my business for £100,000 instead?' he replied, and I recall asking him, 'If we could set up next door for free, why on earth would we pay you £100,000?'

Not that we had the £100,000 anyway but it was true that I could have started up next door for nothing, with all our clients and staff. Eventually we ended up buying the fixtures and fittings from him for £1,750, which we funded with an overdraft from the bank. We also inherited the name Bond Wolfe.

And that's how, two years after graduating from college, I came to own my own business. We were totally naïve and inexperienced. Rory is still my business partner 25 years later, which we are both immensely proud of. The partnership is based on trust and mutual respect, listening intently, particularly when you don't agree, and understanding and believing that your partner has your best interests at heart. Rory's brother Marcus is also the group finance director and a shareholder. His support, trust, expertise and loyalty over the years have been invaluable. I often describe us as a family business with corporate resources. We go out of our way to treat our staff with respect. The rewards of this were brought home to me when my long-suffering PA Lisa, who had joined as an office junior and progressed to partnership status, asked me to be godfather to her daughter, Morgan – something I regarded as a great honour.

The great thing about being totally ignorant, as Rory and I were, is that we had no clue about how hard it would be. I think most people who go into business are blissfully ignorant of that – otherwise they probably wouldn't do it. It is bizarre that if you want to be a car mechanic/

electrician/surgeon you need qualifications, experience and training, but if you want to go into business you can do it without any credentials. This possibly explains why so many businesses fail.

Now that I was self-employed, I realised I had to wise up quite rapidly. I continued to read books about self-development, particularly autobiographies of successful individuals. These helped me realise the importance of goal-setting – daily goals, weekly goals, five yearly, ten yearly. One of my overriding goals was to build up a property portfolio. I had this dream of owning lots of houses. Within 12 or 14 months of buying that first house in 1984, I'd bought another three. I'd raise the deposit, buy the property, get it tenanted and then move on.

Then I decided to sell my first house. To my disappointment, it was only valued at £2,000 more than I'd bought it for and I realised that once I'd deducted estate-agent fees, I'd only be left with a profit of £900 – hardly worth the trouble. Something didn't seem right, so I decided to sell it myself and save the estate agent's fees. I put up a professional 'For Sale' board, and using the company name – Bond Wolfe – I put the house on the market at £5,000 more than it had been valued by the agents. Even then our marketing was so good that people assumed we had been estate agents for years. Then I sat back and waited for the phone to ring. It didn't.

Undeterred, I put up a 'Sold' sign. Within days, other people on the same estate started calling me. 'If you've sold that one for that amount, we want you to sell ours,' they said, and that's how we ended up in the estate agency business. We put many houses on the estate on the market at the same inflated value. If a house was worth £20,000, we'd put it on at £25,000 and because people looked around at the other houses and thought they were worth that amount, that's what they paid for them. To my astonishment, I realised I could not only create a market, but control it as well. And because we'd inflated the local housing market, my own properties also went up in value, which I then sold to release the capital.

Ironically, having gone into this business to avoid paying estate agents' fees, I was now earning money from them. However, there was one difference between me and the other agents: I was getting my clients – and myself – significantly more for their property. But the more I acted as an agent, the more I realised one basic, undeniable fact. As an agent, you get one per cent of the value of a house sale. As an owner you get 99 per cent. I thought, Hang on – I don't want to be Mr One Per Cent. So I started acquiring more properties and went into commercial ones – shops and business premises.

We opened up more estate agency offices and everything was going really well. Then, at the turn of the 1980s, something made me take stock. The market was still really high, but I decided to start selling. I'd never had significant cash before and I had an urge to see some real money. Just after I sold the houses in the late 1980s and early 1990s, interest rates soared and the property market crashed. This was more good luck than a sound financial judgement, although I knew that valuations had gone out of control and instinctively it was time to profit.

Back then, I didn't have any long-term strategy, and I certainly didn't have a crystal ball. I'd have said selling out at the top of the market was pure chance, but when people like me say chance, usually there's a high element of instinct and judgement involved as well. At a time when most people were losing money hand over fist, I was left with £150,000 in cash – a fortune to me at that time.

As prices bottomed out, I started to buy up parades of shops at knock-down rates, offsetting the high interest rates against the rental income. Then, when the interest rates finally started to come down, rents increased, as did the capital values. I remember I bought one building for £400,000 and as the interest rates came down, the rent shot up from £40,000 per year to £80,000 and I sold it for nearly £1million, a fortune at the time. As the early 1990s wore on, we built up a respectable asset base but along with that came quite a lot of media attention, which took a lot of getting used to.

As well as all the properties in West Bromwich, we had an infrastructure of estate agencies in the area that was intended to give us access to market knowledge. The flip-side was that it raised our profile. Without realising it, we had become a big fish in a small pond. For the first time in years, race raised its head again. I kept being referred to as

'Asian' in newspaper reports, yet to me I was Indian. As far as I was concerned, Asian meant Chinese or Japanese.

I'm a private person by nature, and I certainly don't court publicity. If I could have my way, I'd have no public profile at all, but I know the importance of publicity for a company. So right from those early days I played a character called Paul Bassi, who does all the handshaking and the meetings. I set about networking and got involved with a local business chamber, becoming vice president shortly after joining the board. It was a way of keeping on top of what was happening in the wider business community, and this was really the start of our 'giving back' principle. I strongly believe that financial success brings with it the responsibility of supporting those in your community who are less fortunate than you, and we have set up the Bond Wolfe Charitable Trust to deal with this responsibility.

By the late 1990s we had substantial assets by most people's standards, and everyone in the area knew who we were. The more people knew about us, the more opportunities came our way. I'd stopped selling the properties I owned, and instead started remortgaging them to release capital, always fixing our interest rates in order to eliminate our exposure to the potential of rises. With secure access to cash, I was able to react very quickly to changing markets and make highly profitable deals, so our assets and reputation went from strength to strength.

To this day, we aim to be always slightly ahead of the market bandwagon. We want to inhabit the space others aren't in – to get there before everyone else and leave just as they all arrive. I don't rely on inflation, yield compression or good fortune, all of which must be treated as a bonus. You should always establish your strategy and profit objective before you enter a deal and not rely on new sales, seasonal periods or the cyclical 'boom and bust' nature of the world economies.

Looking back, I'm very happy with my life and the choices I've made, apart from that constant inability to enjoy the here and now. Always seeing the bigger picture means you're constantly thinking ahead of yourself, always one step removed from what's happening in the present. A part of my mind is always feeling responsible for the business, permanently looking ahead out of concern for my children, family and friends. This means I am never carefree. Perhaps my greatest disappointment is that I find it so hard to really enjoy the journey as it happens. In a business context, though, that philosophy has served us very well. We're still in property and we still have significant cash resources, and we make it our business not to chase the market and always able to capitalise on an opportunity. We're on schedule towards my goals.

But growing your business, establishing successful strategies and improving the security, quality, risk and diversity of your business also require an extensive quality network. Somewhere along the way I have been fortunate to establish mutually beneficial key influential relationships with an exceptional number of leading entrepreneurs, professionals, financial institutions, government bodies and senior politicians, locally and nationally. I don't go out of my way to court these contacts, they just seem to have happened, but I absolutely respect their value. Occasionally I'll read myself described as one of the 'best connected businessmen of his generation', which is gratifying but confusing, as I still see myself as that little Indian boy from a very orthodox Sikh family.

Over the years of running our business, I've learned so many things about how to make a company work, but the main ingredient of success, as I'll never tire of saying, is that you can never overestimate the value of goal-setting. I have annual goals and what I call 'big picture' goals. I've recorded and kept every goal I ever set myself – everything from buying a new suit to buying a car or a property, getting my children educated, or travel and fitness. I used to have limiting beliefs – that there was a limitation to what I could achieve in my life. Now I realise the only limitations are those we put on ourselves. The goals I have today are more substantial and varied than before, but the hunger to achieve them has increased.

People sometimes ask me what motivates me to keep going, now that I've got everything I want in my life. The truth is I keep going because I can and I want to. I'd feel that I had failed if I didn't fulfil my full potential, and I don't feel comfortable with failure. I want to set an example to my three children and three nephews, so that they fulfil their enormous potential. My parents wanted to provide for their family. They wanted us to have nice things, but didn't see any value in education, whereas I want my children and nephews to have the education and experience to appreciate their lifestyle and understand the responsibility that comes with it.

My family and closest friends give me balance. My brothers Kamal and Tim have always been totally supportive and as a family, we have a 'we are strong like mountains' motto. In my wife Priya, I'm with someone who is happy with the person I am and who understands my complex mindset, gives me space and total support.

It would be inaccurate to say I'm constantly striving to achieve more as a way of proving something to others. I don't feel I have to prove anything to myself or anyone else. That's not what motivates me. I want to be able to pass on to the next generations a substantial business, a legacy and responsibility that will give them and the generations ahead, a good life. Of course my son Bobby and my daughters Terri and Nikita, together with my nephews Gurpreet, Paul and George, may not want to come into the business. They might want to be florists, artists or poets, and if that's the case, good luck to them – I would absolutely support them. If they do choose to go into the business they wouldn't be able to take on any senior responsibilities within the company until they'd done a ten-year apprenticeship in and out of the business. My children and nephews are fortunate. But with that privilege comes responsibility and varying challenges.

But it's not only my children and nephews who keep me going. It's also the fear of losing what I've built up, and particularly the luxury of choice. I'm lucky enough to have absolute choice over what I do. If I want to do something, I do it. If I want a new car, to go on holiday, to make a donation to charity or take a day off to be with my family and friends, I don't think about it – I just do it. That's one of the greatest gifts that money can give you – that autonomy over what you do – and the fear of losing it really motivates me to keep going.

But my life is not all about money and material choices. There's a spiritual side to it that comes from my grandmother, who was very religious. I go to the Sikh temple once a week and I say a prayer each and every time I come in or go out of my house, when I sleep and when I wake. This probably originates from spending weekends at the temple with my grandmother, from the age of six until I was about 12. My faith gives me enormous peace of mind and I believe that spiritual element is so important, particularly when you're surrounded by wealth, material motives, power, politics and egos. I know that whatever I give out, I'll get back. I don't take advantage of people and I always try to treat everyone fairly and with respect. I truly believe that if you're good at what you do, and you treat people well, you'll be rewarded.

There is nothing difficult or mysterious about success. All the successful people I know are exactly the same as everyone else – they argue with their kids over homework, they have two arms and two legs. The only difference between them and the next guy is that they think bigger – they set their finishing line further. I always say to people, 'If you're going to have a plan, make it a big plan, a different plan.' When everyone else was buying a few properties, I bought the street.

I don't believe in luck but I respect it. I believe every person is exactly who they want to be. If you are unsuccessful and are jobless long term, that's because you want to be that way. Otherwise you'd be something different. It's a hard stance to take, but a true one. It's about changing the way you think. You have to want success and you have to believe you can get it. It's that old adage – if you conceive it and believe it, you'll achieve it. I absolutely believe that. Success is not somebody else's domain.

And you have to keep going, no matter what knock-backs you get. Life isn't a continual up. We have down days, and we've weathered the same recessions as everyone else and encountered the same problems. But the difference is that, as long as you've got a bigger picture in your head of where you want to be, you won't pack up at the first sign of stormy weather. You'll just get out the brolly and wait it out. The key to weathering the storm is surrounding yourself with quality people, family, friends, colleagues, staff and advisors, and reading your marketplace.

It's true that my life is pretty stressful. Most people would have a breakdown if they experienced just one month in my life, but to me it's just my world. I can lose a lot of money one day and still go home and say hello to my wife and kids, turn on the telly and play about with the remote control like most men. If I took all the knocks to heart, I wouldn't last a minute. Ups and downs are an inevitable part of life. I don't throw lavish parties when there are highs, and I don't sit and cry in a corner when we're going through the lows. If I lose one battle I don't whinge. I just get on with it.

When things are tough I know there's a steel rod running through the middle of me. Most of the time it's well hidden but when there's a challenge, I always step up to meet it. In some ways I thrive on pressure. I always come up with a plan. I'm simply not prepared to allow anything to knock me off my course. As a leader, you have to show leadership and your staff have to have confidence and belief in you. Even when you may be under pressure, you should never show it. That's the thing about successful people – they grow under pressure, while unsuccessful people shrivel. In fact, pressure can become like a drug. I'm always saying I'm going to take time off and swan about in Spain, but after a few days I'm back in the office. I just can't live without it. There will be a time to take it easy but not for another 20 years.

Looking back, I've always had that self-belief. It probably dates back to when I was playing sports at school. Whenever I walked out onto a pitch, I never entertained the possibility that we could lose. That's not to say you should be self-deluded. If you deceive yourself in business or any other aspect of life, you're on a slippery slope. You have to be brutally honest with yourself about your strengths and your limitations.

I've read a lot about success and achievement, and there are certain basic rules you must adhere to.

- You've got to want it. Desire, not ability, determines success, and you can win only if you want to. You must learn from your mistakes: win wars not battles. Don't let money be your motivating factor. Money is simply a way of measuring success. What you should really aspire to is choice and freedom. Money is and always will be a by-product of success. Successful people do not chase money.
- To really understand the game, sometimes you have to step off the field and observe from the sidelines. Nowadays I probably spend 70 per cent of my time there.
- Work hard and play hard. The harder you work, the luckier you will get and remember there is no such thing as coincidence.
  Strike a balance in your life. You can't afford to be over-obsessive about work. Avoid burn-out, and love your family and friends.
- Adopt a quality mentor, surround yourself with good people, and respect everyone. You will not plan to fail, but you can fail to plan.
- Listen aggressively, and read and learn all the time. Be

highly knowledgeable in your chosen field and mix with your outstanding peers. That is the only way you will make real progress.

- Trust your instinct, and stick to the 'knitting' – stick to and specialise in what you know best.
  Finally, never give up. Believe in yourself and your big picture, and keep replacing your goals.

Success happens incrementally, like children growing up. To me, life is all about being a good human being, living a great life before you go to meet your maker, making an outstanding contribution to the people in your life, and having no personal regrets.

CHAPTER 3

KIM EINHORN
SAY YES FIRST AND
PANIC LATER

Kim Einhorn, 52, and her brother David run the phenomenally successful Theme Traders, one of the world's leading event-organising and prop-hire companies. Not bad for a pair who started out entertaining at children's parties as The Red Elephant and Spaceman Sam...

It was all looking a bit hairy. In one corner cowered a belly dancer with a large snake wrapped around her, while in another stood an irate rat catcher surrounded by, well, rats. Between them was a palpable wall of tension. When I'd had the inspired idea to book both acts to appear at the same party, I'd overlooked one simple fact. Snakes eat rats.

There's one thing you can say about being a party organiser — it's never, ever dull. Which is just as well really, because ever since I was a child I've had a really low boredom threshold. At school in north London, I had a reputation for being disruptive as I had real problems sitting down and focusing. I caused quite a lot of chaos, but then I think creative people do tend to be quite disruptive. I was always in trouble because my skirt was too short or I talked too much. I was always thinking outside of the box.

The teachers couldn't cope with me at all and decided I

must be thick. My father used to go in and tell them, 'You only want to keep her down because she's bored, not because she's stupid.' Not surprisingly, I left school at 15 and went to work for my father. At that time, in the mid-1970s, he ran a shop in London called Laurence Corner, which sold army surplus stuff – naval tops, army shirts, jodpurs, hats, gloves, scarves – anything that came out of the services. It became very famous very quickly and all the big names of the time – The Beatles, Jacqueline Bisset – shopped there.

My older brother, David, was already working there when I joined. Dad had said to him, 'If you can get ten O levels, I'll let you leave school. When David got 11, my father had no choice but to let him leave.

There were two sections to Laurence Corner, the main one selling government surplus and another 'boutique' section round the corner which was owned by my mother, although she hardly ever went in. That's where I started work. Incredibly for someone who'd had such trouble sticking to anything for long, I would work there for 17 years. It sounds crazy now, but the days just went by almost unnoticed until suddenly I'd been there the best part of two decades.

It was a really busy place, and over the years I helped it diversify into costume and props hire. I loved working there, but it wasn't easy working for my father, particularly after my mother died and he remarried someone almost my age, and my brother and I ended up essentially working for her. David, who has always had a huge social conscience, began putting his energies into a charity he'd set up called

POD.org, which ran parties for children in hospital. It wasn't a huge surprise when he left to focus on them full time.

Without David there, I began to lose focus and feel useless. Things came to a head when I had a huge row with my dad. I wanted to give a bonus to someone who'd done a big job for us, but my dad refused. We had a massive fight and I walked out, saying 'I quit.' Naturally I assumed he'd beg me to come back, but he didn't. Instead, in 1990, I joined forces with David.

In order to do the charity parties David was so committed to, we desperately needed an income, but when we added up what we were equipped to do, it didn't amount to much. I'd left school with no qualifications and had been essentially a shop worker ever since, and David wasn't much better. So we decided to become children's entertainers. We developed characters for ourselves – I was the Red Elephant and he was Spaceman Sam. We used to appear at birthday parties and children's events and we were a big hit. Soon parents started asking us to run the entire party for them, so we started organising parties, working out of my garage.

The next bit was a complete fluke, as the best chances in life often are. While I was at Laurence Corner I'd met a guy who worked at TVam and I'd done a job hanging curtains for him. He knew I was organising parties and got in touch with me to say they were doing a big fairground-themed adults party at Alexandra Palace in north London. I was invited to a meeting with 13 or 14 people and I sussed out very quickly that all I had to do was say yes to everything. So even though I knew I was way out of my depth, I volunteered to do everything they were suggesting.

After the meeting I rang David and said, 'I need to set up a fairground inside Ally Pally. Can you help?' Luckily, David isn't easily thrown. We started looking around for defunct fairgrounds and when we realised we weren't going to find one, we decided to build the whole thing in our back garden. As Alexandra Palace had once burned down, everything had to be flame retardant and we painstakingly painted each part by hand on my kitchen table. Then we set about recruiting the fairground 'staff'. We put an ad for performers in *The Stage* magazine and went to interview them in a pub. We needed tarot readers, fairground workers, anything that would bring edge and colour. In the event, the party was a big success and we had loads of letters saying how wonderful it was. That gave us the confidence to think that maybe we could actually do this for a living.

By this stage I was married, conveniently enough, to a diamond dealer. He very kindly lent me £5,000 and a filofax to get the business started properly. We started doing adult parties as well as the children's ones – earning £250 per party and doing an average of two a week. Five hundred pounds a week split between two wasn't huge, but we worked from my house for two years so we didn't have huge outgoings.

Next we set about acquiring props. Whenever we did a party with a certain theme, we'd make the props or scenery we needed and keep them afterwards. It wasn't long before the garage was packed, so we rented another garage, and then another. Over the next few years, we acquired 40 garages and ended up paying £400 a week in rent. By 2001, it was obvious we needed to buy somewhere of our own.

Our first premises was an old dance hall in Cricklewood, which was a bit of a dive. It cost £140,000 – a fortune to us – and we needed a massive mortgage. On the day we were supposed to exchange, the bank withdrew. The manager simply couldn't see the bigger picture and how we were going to make it work. Nowadays event management is big business, but back then we were in an industry no one knew anything about. We had to try to find another bank to fund us, but then our bank also refused to release the £15,000 we had with them, and eventually we had to threaten legal action to get them to release our own funds. From that day on, we realised that everything we wanted, we were going to have to fight for.

As the company expanded and we acquired more and more props, we needed more and more space, so we went on to buy the old place next door and then Turpin's Yard – a site with 11 warehouses. Eventually we also bought a farm in Leighton Buzzard, to the north of London, which is full of containers and is where we keep all our mass items – like the 150 sofas we've accrued. We also have a plant in Scotland.

But it hasn't happened without a huge amount of graft. We were really busy from the word go. Once we'd taken on the mortgage we knew we had to start making serious money. We were still doing the parties – we'd say yes to anything that came along. I think that's really important in business – don't think too hard about anything before committing to it or you'll end up not doing it. If you think too deeply about things, they just won't happen. So I'd drive to Birmingham to do a make-up job that would pay just £75, and David would drive for two hours to entertain at a Harvester. We worked so hard so we were never in a situation where we couldn't pay the mortgage.

People think being a party organiser is glamorous. Let me tell you, that's a very long way from the truth. When you're building up a business, you've got to be prepared to do everything yourselves. I remember sitting down and hand-making 20 pairs of chaps. We made and hired out costumes, and got into party decorations. We did all the rigging and de-rigging of parties, which meant getting there early to set up and going back at two or three in the morning when all the guests had left. It was exhausting. One night I turned up around 2.30am to de-rig and I passed this guy wandering down the road, clasping a giant silver boot. 'Oi!' I shouted, winding the window down. 'I rather think that's mine!'

Gradually we took on more staff, and we now have about 50 or 60 – more if we're doing a big event. People do tend to stay with us an awfully long time, and we still have the very first staff member we hired, which must be a good thing. We're still really hands on even now, and we still say yes to absolutely everything.

People have always had parties, but event organising on a

big scale has only really taken off in the past few years. We were really fortunate to get in at the beginning and we've built up some amazing clients over the years. We used to do all the launches for Iron Maiden, which was a riot. The manager used to say to me, 'Do whatever you like.' That's my kind of client. So we really went to town. One time we recreated the whole of Soho inside a venue. It was crazy. At one party at a hotel the mud wrestlers failed to turn up, so I had to grab two of the lifeguards from the pool. When the original wrestlers did eventually turn up I told them they were too late. If you want to be taken seriously, you have to honour your commitments. That's one thing I've learned.

I love the diversity of my job. No two days are ever quite the same. You could never, ever get bored here. We had one man who came in on a Wednesday and said he was having a big party at Skibo Castle (where Madonna and Guy Ritchie held their wedding bash, in the far north of Scotland) the coming Saturday. He wanted to turn the cellars into a burlesque palace. What did we say? Yes, of course. Saying yes has become so ingrained now, I wouldn't know how to say anything else.

David and I are very much grafters. We're very aware that no one ever gives you anything on a plate and, as clichéd as it sounds, you're only as good as your last job. You have to perform time after time after time. We just don't do second rate. Just because we're financially secure now, it doesn't change that basic hunger to do things properly. Every year we set goals for ourselves for what we want to achieve over the coming year. One year it might be getting on top of health and safety, the following year it might be dealing with surplus stock. It helps to be constantly working towards something. You have to always stay focused on the fact you need a living and you need to do your best 100 per cent of the time. Sure, people will knock you – they always do when you're making a success of something – but it doesn't matter. The thing that matters is that you enjoy what you do.

One of the key things I learned when I was starting out is how essential it is to instil confidence in whoever it is you're talking to. It's that old 'fake it til you make it' thing. Convincing the other person that you're completely confident in yourself is half the battle, even if you then go home and panic. When we were building that initial fairground, a guy came to look around and he was so shocked because we didn't have premises, we were just doing it at my house. I think I'd given the impression we were some hugely slick operation. The first year we did the Christmas grotto at Whiteleys shopping centre in west London, we talked our way into it – convincing them we were just the people for the job, even though we'd never done anything like that before. It *is* possible to turn a fantasy into a reality – you just have to have belief in yourself.

These days the company turns over £4–5million a year, and we've got a property portfolio worth in the region of £15million. It's hard to believe all that stemmed from the Red Elephant and Spaceman Sam! We've got three deputy directors now, and we're training people so that at some stage David and I can step back. Well, that's the theory anyway. But companies need leadership and drive. We're constantly trying to maintain the highest quality and keep our service personal at the same time. Our main dream is to become a legend in the party industry. We have to be all things to all people – support services, party organisers, TV prop suppliers, costumiers. It's hard to juggle everything. At first we imagined we'd have all this old stuff and just sit back and hire it out, but we keep generating more and more new stuff, so storage is an ongoing problem. But there's always variety and diversity, which is what we thrive on. For Elton John's birthday bash we ended up making 100 livery outfits in powder blue. Like I said, we'll do anything.

It's funny looking back to all those years I spent working for my dad in his shop. He never once admitted he'd been wrong to let me go, but that's OK. I'm able to acknowledge now all the things he did give David and me – like our unstoppable energy. That certainly came from him. At the end of the day, we're traders at heart – that's why we're called Theme Traders – and we've got our father to thank for that.

www.podcharity.org.uk runs 2,000 parties a year in hospitals and hospices to bring fun and laughter to sick children

CHAPTER 4

BEN WAY
SELF BELIEF IS ALL I KNOW

Schoolboy entrepreneur Ben Way was a millionaire at 17, but then lost his fortune just as quickly as he'd gained it. Now 27 and head of the corporate and innovation venturing company Rainmakers, he is savouring success second time around.

I was a nightmare child. I was always dismantling things. My parents would come down in the mornings to find I'd taken apart all the plugs. Even at playgroup I had to have constant parental supervision, otherwise I'd crawl under the stage with whatever gadget I could get my hands on and start taking it apart. I just loved the mechanics of it plus, of course, the fact that it was forbidden. Nothing much has changed.

I grew up in a little village in Devon with my sister who was five years younger. My father was an accountant and my mother an artist, but they split up when I was quite young. There was a lot of turbulence and moving about when I was a kid, which probably didn't help calm my already up-and-down nature. I was pretty nuts, to be honest. I'd push things over or run away. One time at my mum's house I chucked an entire bookcase down the stairs. I was just impossible to control. Nowadays I'd probably be diagnosed with something early on – a nice, neat label, or a box to fit me into – but not back then.

I had a love/hate relationship with school. I went to quite a few schools during my childhood; some were good and some were absolutely awful. I always had respect for my teachers – for some reason I always got on really well with adults or people a lot older than me – but I couldn't seem to help being naughty. In class I had friends but I seemed to swing from being really popular to deeply unpopular. I was something of a chameleon and tried to adapt myself to what I thought people wanted from me. But I always had an ability to empathise with other people – to place myself in their shoes and understand what they were thinking and feeling. I think that's really helped me in business, that instinctive intuition about people.

I was always a bit different though, even as a young child. I remember we were all asked what we wanted to be when we were older and all my friends said policeman or footballer. I said I wanted to run my own toy factory. Even then, I saw myself as my own boss. I wasn't a great student at school, but the one thing I was very good at was finding my way around problems and difficult situations. I'd done a bit of amateur dramatics as a teenager, and I persuaded my friend who got all A's in class to write up all his work as a script, and I learned it as an actor would learn lines. I think that's the only way I managed to get nine GCSEs.

My focus was always on the stuff I was doing outside the classroom. When I was nine I was finally diagnosed as dyslexic. In those days hardly anyone had a computer, still less understood how one worked. But I'd seen a computer at my dad's work and, noticing how fascinated I was by it, he wrote to the local authority asking whether I could have one to help me with my written work. Incredibly, a month later, I took delivery of what would now seem the world's biggest, most monstrous laptop. Of course, I thought it was wonderful.

The computer allowed me to take pride in my work for the very first time. Before that, my handwriting had been so appalling that it was almost impossible for anyone to read what I'd written. Now I started to feel good about what I was handing in. I got good at computers very quickly. The dyslexic brain is very logical and I'd always had an affinity with technology, probably stemming from all those hours taking electrical things apart when I was a small child.

This was about 1992 or 1993 and gradually the rest of the world was waking up to the computer age, but I was one step ahead. So when my friends' parents started to get computers and couldn't understand how they worked, they'd call me out to help them. As my reputation spread, I realised I could actually make some money out of this and started charging £10 an hour. Before long I was running a fully-fledged computer consultancy business out of my bedroom and writing software programmes. Working around school timetables, I was probably turning over around £20,000 a year. I ran that business – The Quad Computer Consultancy – for about three years while still at school. It felt right to me to be earning money. I'd always wanted to make a lot of money. It was part of my whole ethos.

Of course things have changed a bit now. It's funny, when I was first earning large sums, people would say to me, 'Money doesn't buy you happiness,' and I always really hated that. But when I lost my fortune, I realised they were right. Money doesn't buy you happiness – but what it does buy you is opportunity, and then it's up to you to turn that opportunity into happiness.

But that was a long way ahead when I first started running my computer company. Right then, all I was concerned with was turning over as much as I could. I suppose after being told for ten years that I was useless at school, I wanted that respect that came from being so good at something people would pay for your services or advice. And that's what computing gave me.

After three years of increasing success and turnover, the media got hold of my story. Suddenly there was a buzz of interest in the story of a schoolboy who was making money running his own business from his bedroom. This interest went through the roof when, in the year after I left school at 16 to work full time, I became a millionaire. I started appearing on chat shows, which I really enjoyed. I like the camera and I like performing. I'm an extrovert – you have to be if you're an entrepreneur – and the spotlight didn't faze me. I was always had this 'youngest millionaire' billing, which felt strange because although I was a millionaire on paper, it wasn't as though I had a million pounds sitting in my bank that I could withdraw at the cash point any time I liked.

After I'd appeared in a Channel 4 documentary, I was approached by some investors based in Jersey, looking for money-making projects to back. 'We've got money,' they told me. 'Have you got ideas?' I didn't really know what I was doing at that stage, so I just plucked a ridiculous figure out of the air and asked for £25million. To my amazement they said, 'That's just the kind of figure we were looking to invest.' At the age of 16 or 17, I'd entered the big league.

Up until that point I'd still been based in the attic of my mum's house in Bath. But suddenly I found myself living in a penthouse apartment in Jersey, complete with four-poster beds and white carpets. It can remember literally pinching myself as I looked around, just to see if it really was real.

As I was so young, there were certain restrictions imposed on me. I couldn't drink or smoke or even have a girlfriend who wasn't vetted by the company. I wasn't too impressed, as you can imagine. I stayed in Jersey a year, but it wasn't a happy time. I was being paid a six-figure salary but I realised that the investors were as interested in my PR value as my technical abilities. Eventually I fell out with the investors, who just weren't prepared to let me have the kind of control I wanted. Despite the beautiful flat and the fancy furniture, I was completely miserable.

One day I'd had enough. I just got on a boat and headed to London. It was Christmas time and I'd never even been to London before, but I knew I had to get away from Jersey.

I stayed in a hotel for a week and then rented a flat. Even though I'd relocated from Jersey, I was still working for the original investors and receiving my huge salary, so I lived the high life, eating at places like The Ivy. With the equity I had in the venture company, I was worth £18million on paper, and I was still only 19. Life was pretty good. In 2000 I won the title of Young Entrepreneur of the Year and through that, I got involved with various government initiatives. Throughout 2001 I travelled extensively to the US to consult on technology. I was even invited to the White House. Being introduced to part of the Clinton administration was one of my proudest moments.

And then the dotcom bubble burst. All of a sudden my pay cheques from the Jersey investors stopped coming in. At first they blamed accountancy errors but finally they said that, out of necessity, they were going to disband the company, rendering my £18million of stock worthless. I was broke. On the same day I read in the paper that my name was on the *Sunday Times* Rich List – number 18, under Robbie Williams – I found myself without even enough money left to buy a tube ticket.

Luckily a really good friend, telecoms boss Chris Moss whom I'd met at the Young Entrepreneur of the Year awards ceremony, came to my rescue. He invited me to stay with him and his family in Berkshire, and I gratefully accepted. They've now become like a second family to me.

It was a really dismal time in my life. I felt like a complete failure. I was terrified the newspapers would get hold of what had happened and expose me as a huge fraud. When you're 19 years old and have got used to being told you're the best thing since sliced bread, you fall hard.

Getting back on my feet after that was a slow and quite painful business. I did nothing for a year, because I had to try to get my confidence back. Only then could I start to think about setting up on my own again. For a while I carried on consulting, then in 2002 I started up a company called Rainmakers. We call ourselves an innovation and corporate venturing company. What that means is that we come up with product ideas – anything that involves technology – and then launch them into the marketplace. It suits me because at heart I'm an inventor. I come up with an idea and put a structure around it.

Starting again from scratch was a bit strange after the success I'd had before. We had very little capital and got cheap offices in Piccadilly. But I didn't really worry about it. When you're in business you have to take the rough with the smooth. I never for a moment felt it wasn't going to work. It'd be like a musician worrying whether he was going to be able to play properly. Business is what I do – it's what my brain is geared towards. It's absolutely second nature to me.

Running a company is multi-tasking in its most extreme form. You have to do so many things at the same time – cash flow, personnel, strategising, marketing. Sure, you can delegate at some point, but you still have to understand how all these things work. We have lots of subsidiary companies which we have an equity stake in, but I've kept

Rainmakers small so that I can maintain control over what we do. Essentially it's just me and my support staff, but it's doing really well and I'm very pleased with it.

I've always known I'd succeed again. It's just been a question of when, rather than if. That might sound arrogant but self-belief is all I know. I've never been scared, so I'm not scared of taking risks. That's the one thing you can't afford if you're running a business. I'll always take the big decisions. When you're running a business you have to make the decision regardless of whether it's right or wrong. Business is a combination of decision-taking and risk-taking. People come to me because I'm not afraid of making decisions. I don't hesitate. Sometimes I get it wrong, but I get it right more than I get it wrong. It's an intuitive thing now. I've been in business so long, it's become my life. I feel the next move naturally.

I'm lucky because, having lost my fortune, I'm now back to multi-million pound status again. I'm not flashy but I have a pretty good lifestyle. Just how good was brought home to me when I took part in the first series of Channel 4's *The Secret Millionaire*. When they first approached me I said no, on the basis that it felt pretentious and wrong for a rich guy to give poor people money. But then they convinced me it was a risk worth taking, so I went undercover to help out at the Pedro Youth Club in Hackney's 'Murder Mile'. It really helped me develop an understanding of the social problems we face. My own childhood was challenging in certain respects, so I had some common ground with the people there but I was shocked at the way they all seemed to feel they had to fight over everything. I ended up donating £25,000 to the centre and I'm now on the board of trustees of the club. I think it's crazy that initiatives like this, which play a huge role in reducing crime in their neighbourhoods, don't receive better funding.

Nowadays I don't like to make long-term plans. I enjoy the randomness of my business, and the fact I have no idea what we're going to be doing next. I've always done things in that intuitive way, so I couldn't give a format for entrepreneurial success, but I do have some general advice for anyone who wants to set up any kind of business:

- Business is simpler than you imagine. It's mostly about people. If you understand people, you understand business.
- There'll never be a 'right time' to start a business. If you wait until everything's perfect, you'll be waiting for ever. Just go for it. Take the plunge.
- Don't be afraid of failure. Even if you fail, you'll learn more in the short time you're running the business than you would in a lifetime of reading about it. My failure has definitely made me a better person. I'm a better human being. I don't take myself so seriously. Fear should never be a reason for not starting a business. Whatever happens, you'll learn some really important life skills.

- Starting a business requires a huge amount of passion. It has to be the most important thing in your life. You have to love what you do and you have to love the people you work with. Everything else will fall into place.
- Remember Occam's Razor: all things being equal, the simplest explanation is usually the right one.

CHAPTER 5

DAME MARY PERKINS
WORK, WORK, WORK

With her husband, Douglas, Dame Mary Perkins has built up her optician's business from a cramped room above a Bristol shop to the global chain Specsavers. Now 64 and reportedly worth £500million, she has no intention of standing down – not while there's still so much to be done.

It's always a strange feeling to open the papers and read that I'm supposed to be worth all these huge sums of money. To be honest, it doesn't actually mean anything, because you're only worth that amount of money if someone buys your company for that amount of money. Besides, our company is private so it's all complete guesswork on behalf of the journalists who compile those Rich Lists.

In the end wealth is just a number. There's nothing magical about it. Yes, if my washing machine broke down, I'd be able to replace it without worrying, but I still drive around in the two-seater MG ZB I've had for ten years. Most of the time, in fact, I cycle to work. And I'm certainly not a big spender on clothes or jewellery. Probably that's down to my childhood, which nowadays would appear to have been very austere, though at the time it was just ordinary.

I was born in Bristol in 1944. At the time my father was in

the Navy and I spent the first few years of my life living with my grandparents. When my father was finally demobbed in 1948 we moved into a prefab house. These were supposed to be makeshift temporary structures to ease the chronic post-war housing crisis, but to my mother it was heaven. At last she had her own inside loo. We were there for a couple of years until, six months after my mother gave birth to my younger brother, everything changed. Tragically, my father's sister and her husband died from influenza within days of one another, leaving their three young sons orphaned. Overnight our family almost doubled as they came to live with us. Clearly the prefab was no longer sufficient.

We were moved into a council house on the outskirts of Bristol. My mother loved it because it was large and modern and our estate bordered on the countryside. My father, who'd come from a very hard-working cotton mills background, found a job working in a chemist shop, where much of his time was spent delivering the medicines. At the same time, he took advantage of a new scheme on offer from the new National Health Service to fast-track ex-servicemen through their optometry qualifications to make up for a nationwide shortage of opticians. For three years, he'd work in the chemist's during the day and then go to night school in the evenings. Eventually, to the family's great pride, he qualified as an optometrist, opening his own little shop.

Mine was a very ordinary post-war childhood. We'd go off into the countryside on our bikes or just play in the street outside. By modern standards, we had very little – no telephone, no TV, but then neither did anyone else we knew, so it didn't seem as though we were missing out on anything. It was the 1950s and everyone more or less did what they were told. I was quite a good little girl. I helped my mother out – with four boys in the house, she needed all the help she could get. Sometimes my friends and I would go to the church youth club or occasionally to a coffee shop – that was about the most daring thing I could think of to do. We didn't have a car so we had to get buses everywhere, which severely curtailed my social life.

I passed my eleven-plus and even though I wasn't particularly brainy, I went on to study physics and maths at A level, already knowing that I was going to be an optician. It was quite unusual in those days for girls to study science subjects, but it was what my parents expected of me. I think they just assumed I would follow in my dad's footsteps. I suppose I probably was quite ambitious because once I realised I had to do sciences in order to study optics, I knuckled down and got on with it, even though I'd have loved to have done something like English. I'm always reading about young entrepreneurs now and how they started buying and selling things and making money at a very young age, but I didn't do any of that. In the 1950s you were just pleased if you could pass your exams and have a bit of normal fun.

To study optometry I went to Cardiff University, where I met my husband Douglas on my first day. I suppose it must have been fate. We've been inseparable ever since. I was one of only three girls on my course and I think growing up in a household of boys really helped me hold my own in that environment – as well as later on, when I went into what was then a very male business.

I left university in 1965 and finished my pre-registry year (a kind of work placement with a registered optometrist prior to qualifying) in 1967. At that time, most optometrists went to work for a big chain – at that time the biggest was Dollond & Aitchison – or an independent opticians. So I was unusual in that I decided to set up on my own. My father had always worked on his own, so it was what I was used to, but in retrospect it was a little daunting. There weren't so many regulations in those days. I learned about things like book-keeping on the job as I went along.

I started my business in the late-1960s. It was called Bebington, which was my maiden name. In fact, it was well into the 1980s before I started using my married name of Perkins. I worked from a room above a baker's shop, and shared a waiting room with the doctor who had the room next door. Douglas, who'd also qualified as an optometrist, had a different room near the Bristol market. We both set up on a shoestring. We'd inherited some equipment from my father, who'd retired by this point, and there wasn't any big financial outlay involved. There were no shop windows or anything. In those days you did what you did within the limits of whatever you had – you didn't go getting big loans or anything.

Looking back, we worked incredibly hard, but at the time it was just how things were. My father had always taught me that I'd have to work for a living and that no one would ever hand me anything on a plate, so I knew financial security wasn't going to fall from a tree and land in my lap. It would be a question of grafting for it.

In the meantime Douglas and I had got married. For the first two years we lived in a bedsit, but when my daughter (the first of our three children) was born at the end of 1967, we bought a house. It was a detached three-bedroom corner house with a garage and it cost us £4,000 – a huge sum at the time, even with a mortgage. For someone who'd grown up on a council estate, buying a house was a really big deal and the pair of us were scared stiff. Of course we had nothing to go in it apart from some old curtains my mother-in-law had going spare, so we had to go to a furniture warehouse to get the basics.

Once we had the house, both of us worked from there on a Sunday, as well as having working from our respective rooms during the week. The people waiting to have their eyes tested would take turns in rocking the baby. In addition, we worked together on different premises three nights a week, and we did that for three years. So we were effectively working Monday to Friday, Sunday mornings and three nights a week. The hours were really long, but somehow it didn't seem hard. The pair of us were used to working hard and we accepted that was how things were. When I had my second daughter it got a bit tougher, but I managed to get the daughter of a friend to move in and help with child care.

Before long my husband and I joined forces, using shared premises that became known as Bebington and Perkins. Almost from the first day we were making good money. We started that first business in 1967 and by 1980 we had a chain of 23 shops spread around the West Country. We'd never set out to become moguls, but those were the days of astronomical taxation, and one of the ways to save paying high taxes was to keep reinvesting profits in opening new businesses. So we did.

In 1980, we decided we'd gone as far as we wanted in that particular field and sold the chain of shops to Dolland & Aitchison for the princely sum of £2million. Two million pounds was a huge amount of money in those days. It just didn't seem real, to be honest. One of the terms of the sale was that we couldn't work in the field of optics for three years, so we decided to take a break and move to Guernsey, where my parents were then living, to try to work out what to do next.

It was a strange time, because we never intended to stay in Guernsey yet that's what we wound up doing. People often think we live there because of the tax situation, but the truth is we really did end up there by accident. In fact, we actually paid tax on the sale of our business and then moved to Guernsey, which proves just how un-tax-savvy we were! The children moved to schools in Guernsey, we bought a lovely house and we tried to keep ourselves occupied. I went to work at the Citizens Advice Bureau, just for something to do, but Douglas found it very hard not being able to work. He went a bit doo-lally, to be honest.

I suppose we could have decided never to work again, but it never really crossed our minds. We were still in our thirties and work was all we knew. I also didn't think it would be a good example to set the children, not to see us working. I worried they'd become work-shy, but I think I've tipped them the other way – the three of them are workaholics!

Despite the £2million from the sale of the business, we really didn't live the high life – we still don't. Most of the money went on the house and school fees, and we didn't really splash out on anything else. We've always kept our cars until they fall apart – no point doing anything else really on an island where things rust so quickly.

In 1984, more or less as soon as the three years specified in the sale were up, we started Specsavers. It was conceived as a joint venture between us and individual opticians under a general Specsavers umbrella. We'd provide the support services – marketing, payroll, warehousing the frames – but the optometrists would run their own stores. At that time, the strict regulations surrounding the optics industry had just been relaxed. We were now allowed to advertise products and services, and the new business took advantage of that. We'd thought we'd probably build up a bigger chain than we'd had before but never in our wildest dreams could we have predicted how successful the business would become. We've now got more than 600 stores in the UK and taken the brand abroad, which is something I'd never have envisaged.

I've always been hands on and led from the front. At first we were working so hard we didn't see how huge it was getting, but by the early 1990s we were starting to feel financially and economically secure as a company. We had a world-class board of specialists and even the fast rate of expansion still felt comfortable. It was also great fun.

Today the business still keeps growing stronger and we're constantly looking for new ways to expand. But I think when you're brought up with the kind of work ethic I was, you never really sit back and think, Now I'll live the good life. True, I fly first class whenever I go to Australia, two weeks out of every eight, but that's really so that I'm not so jetlagged and can work properly. We don't drive new cars or go off on flash holidays. In fact, the kind of holidays I tend to go on are walking trips with friends where we stay in nice pubs that offer good food.

I'm 64 now and people have started hinting that I might be thinking about retiring, but the truth is I'm having too much fun at work. All three of my children work within the company, so it's very much a family concern. I've got seven grandchildren now, and I'm very much hoping that at least one of them might also follow suit, but you can't force these things. In the meantime, I still love what I do. Expanding into different countries has brought its own challenges and excitement. I'm spending time with lots of different people, most of them younger, which is very refreshing. Besides, what else would I do? Sit at home and knit? I don't think so somehow.

CHAPTER 6

WILLIAM BERRY
THE ENTREPRENEURIAL
MINDSET

*William Berry, who won the BT Essence of the
Entrepreneur Award in 2006 at the age of 29, believes
entrepreneurs are born, not made. Now head of several
web-based businesses, including Net121 and
Accommodation for Students, he has been running
businesses since he was 11 years old.*

When I was about eight years old, my grandparents were round at our house playing cards with my parents in the living room. I think they all thought I'd gone to bed, but in fact I was in the garage with my older brother, who was taking his old Land Rover to bits. Despite my help, nothing was working and he was getting in an increasingly filthy mood, so about 1am I decided to call it a day. Trudging through the living room, covered in grease and thoroughly fed up, I paused to throw a look of weary resignation at the startled card-players. 'It's obvious that someone in this family is going to have to make some money,' I sighed. 'And it looks like it's going to have to be me.'

I was born with the kind of entrepreneurial mindset that would have thrived in an urban environment. However, Bourton-on-the-Water in Gloucestershire, where I grew up, was anything but urban. The nearest proper town was 16 miles away. I had to nurture my business aspirations in complete isolation.

My mum was a housewife and my dad an insurance salesman, so I wasn't really exposed to any entrepreneurial role models. Every now and then you'd see someone like Richard Branson on the news, but it seemed a million miles away from where I lived out in the middle of nowhere. Yet I always felt something like a calling to set up a business. You could almost call it a vocation. It's like a sailor feeling the pull of the sea.

My first business venture was a shop, which I set up in the double garage of our house when I was about 11. In the summer our village was full of tourists, and our garage opened out onto a popular car park, so there were a lot of potential customers. I was given a load of out-of-date stock from a bookshop that was closing down, so I set to work with a friend flogging tourist guides written eight years earlier and obscure biographies of people no one had ever heard of. I think we made about £40.

Swept away by the dizzying success of this first venture, I decided to extend my empire. My mum used to make things out of stained glass and I started using her leftover bits to make my own things – stars and parrots. They definitely had that hand-made look, but still I managed to persuade some local shops to stock them. One of my proudest moments was when I was walking to school past one of those shops and I saw one of my stars in the window. I really felt such a sense of achievement.

Whenever I saw an opportunity for making some money, I took it. Any school fete would find me setting up some kind of stall or other. I remember hearing about a competition to encourage young entrepreneurs. The aim was to see who could raise the most money in a set period of time. I persuaded the school library to let us use the premises to turn into a games arcade. I got all my mates to bring in their PlayStation consoles and we charged other kids to come in and use them. We made a fortune – well, a few hundred quid anyway.

There was never really any doubt about what I wanted to study when I left school. At 18 I left the sticks behind and went to Manchester University to study business and marketing. After all my years in the middle of nowhere, it was such a pleasure to be around people who thought the same way as me, and to exchange ideas. Always on the look-out for money-making schemes, I got together with university friends to start running nightclub evenings and events.

To be honest, I probably overdid the partying that first year. City life was such a culture shock for me that I over-indulged. So after my first year, I decided I needed to get clean away for the summer and clear my head. There was a guy in the library handing out leaflets about being a salesman in America. Perfect, I thought. It would give me a break from all the bad influences at home, plus I'd get to hone a few business skills and learn about a new culture at the same time.

Well, not exactly. The job was selling books door to door. The training was in Nashville. That part was great: lots of whooping and hollering and high fives. Sadly, it was all downhill from there. A bunch of us were sent to the same area – Beaver County, Ohio – and told, 'Go around knocking on doors until you find someone who'll put you up.' They gave us some sample books to lug around and show people, but you weren't allowed to give those out. Instead people were expected to pay money to order books they wouldn't get until the end of the summer. That was a hard sell. In fact, I got an awful lot of rejection. One guy even chased me off his porch with a shotgun. The only sales I made were more out of pity than good salesmanship, I fear.

When I eventually came back a couple of months later, I'd paid for my trip and made a tiny bit of money. But I had also learned some basic rules about selling, which have stood me in good stead ever since. We were taught the seven basic steps: preparation, introduction, questioning, presentation, overcoming objections, close and follow-up. Once you understand those fundamental principles, you can apply them to any kind of sale. I've never forgot them.

Back in Manchester, I was itching to get into the next venture, so in 1999 four of us decided to set up Net 121, a web marketing business. At that time, no one knew a thing about web design or web marketing. Certainly the four of us were pretty clueless, but we could tell it was going to be a burgeoning industry and we wanted to get in at the beginning.

I started going to a business networking event called First Tuesday, which basically put you in touch with people in the business world. There I bumped into a journalist who was supposed to be writing a piece profiling an up-and-coming entrepreneur for the *Manchester Evening News*. To cut a long story short, she ended up writing it about me and the company, and it was read by someone at Granada TV who thought we'd be good for a programme they wanted to make about a new business.

We had no premises, and only one or two clients we'd got through word of mouth from people we'd met doing work placements at university, but suddenly this woman rang and said they wanted to make a TV programme about us – a day in the life of our business. Fair enough. Then she said, 'We'll want to film you in your office.' Gulp.

Even while I was saying no problem, I was trying to think of a way around it. Eventually we managed to borrow an empty office for a day. Then we got all our mates to come in with their computers and stay there the whole day, pretending to be engaged on company business. In the end, the film basically consisted of a few minutes of me talking to the camera, with lots of people looking busy behind me, but it brought us a massive response and got us an instant reputation in the business world. That taught me a really important early lesson about the value of free publicity and marketing – and just how essential good PR can be.

In 2000 I left university and was faced with a choice of taking a job or running Net 121. The dotcom bubble was still rising, so I decided to take the job option, figuring that Net 121 would keep ticking along in the background for a while. I found a job with an American dotcom company based in London. The job title was Junior Project Manager, but when I turned up for work on the first day, I discovered my immediate boss had been fired. 'Who'll be the new Senior Project Manager, then?' I asked.

'You,' was the reply.

Rule number one in business: never show you're panicking! I went straight in to lead a team of eight people. It was a steep learning curve, but I learned an awful lot about managing people, projects and dealing with business politics. After a year there, I moved on to a consultancy company to advise on dotcom and internet businesses – and was still keeping my oar in with Net 121.

Rule number two in business: it's good to diversify. In 2001, I launched Accommodation for Students, a web-based property site that matched students looking for accommodation with landlords looking for tenants. That has been very successful. In 2003, I moved into conference venues, launching Conferences UK. Then finally in 2005 I started up Thomas Charles – a venue-finding service that has proved immensely successful. When I sold it a couple of years ago, it was worth £12million.

Suddenly I had a million in my pocket and another couple of million on the way. I decided to invest some and blow some. Until then I'd been living quite a frugal existence in a flat in a not-very-glamorous part of London. It was lovely to be able to splash out. I bought an Aston Martin and moved into Mayfair in central London. It's true that money doesn't buy you happiness, but what it does buy is security – and that's a really valuable commodity.

After that I went back to focusing on Net 121. By that

stage, I'd really come to understand the business I was in, and that's so important. No matter how many companies you're involved in, fundamentally you need to understand your business and your business model. My role in each of my companies is basically the same – I deal with strategy and web systems. What I learn from one business I then apply to another. I usually look for business partners who are detail-oriented, because that's certainly not my strong point. I do a lot of networking and through that I meet interesting people and if they're passionate about something, I know they're likely to make a good business partner. I'm not the world's greatest salesman, so I've tended to get other people within the company to take over that side of things.

All my companies have started out slowly and grown organically, which means I've had the chance to make small mistakes along the way and learn from them. I think that's better than starting off with a huge chunk of money, which exposes you to the risk of making more and bigger mistakes. Now I've got quite a nice stable of companies and businesses, and that suits me fine. I'll keep on diversifying gradually and getting into slightly bigger ventures, but I'll stick to the basic business model I've used all along. Here are some important lessons I've learned:

- Learning to deal with knock-backs is a huge part of sticking around in business. It can be really tough when you've worked hard on something and you don't get the contract, even though you know you're better than the competition. But you have to learn from those rejections, and understand what it means to keep going out and competing no matter what.

- If you want to do something, don't think too long and hard about it – just go out there and do it. There's no point in talking endlessly about it, or it just won't get done.

- When you're in business it's imperative to be completely honest with yourself. You need to know who you are and to know your own limitations.

- Another key thing I've learned is the value of having the right business partner on board. It has to be someone you trust and someone who complements your skills, but it's probably best not to work with friends. In my case, the original four people I started Net 121 with left quite soon after graduation and I took over the company. It's just better to keep business and social life apart.

It's funny now thinking back to that time when I was selling out-of-date books from my mum and dad's garage. But then maybe it's not that much of a huge leap. At the end of the day it's all about seizing opportunities when they come your way. And it's about confidence, and getting that confidence across to other people so they feel they want to invest in whatever product or service you're selling. Come to think of it, there might still be a box or two of those old books kicking around my parents' house. Sorry, Dad!

CHAPTER 7

NIGEL GOLDMAN

THAT FIRE IN THE BELLY

*He made millions and lost them — twice. Now, with
two spells in prison behind him, 51-year-old Nigel
Goldman — commodities trader, author and gambler — is
uniquely placed to offer insight into how to find success
without losing perspective.*

L ooking back at my life, I've had everything I've ever
wanted. I've had the best cars, I've travelled the world,
stayed in the greatest hotels and eaten at the finest
restaurants. I've done things most people only dream of. But
you know what? I'll never get to a point where I think to
myself, OK, I've done it all now − that's enough. I'll never
get to the stage where I think it's time to take it easy.
Because once you lose that fire in the belly, that urge to keep
on succeeding no matter what, it's all over. You've given up.

Perhaps my motivation to keep going is down to having
made spectacular amounts of money − and lost it all, not
once but twice. I know how it feels to be poor and I know
how it feels to be rich and believe me, I know which I
prefer. Or perhaps, even after all these years, I'm still trying
to prove something − to show my childhood detractors
who thought they were better than me because they had
more money how wrong they were.

I grew up in Birmingham, the only son of hardworking Jewish parents. My father was a dentist and my mother assisted him. It was a comfortable life until I reached the age of eight and my parents decided they wanted to send me to a boarding school. I got a scholarship to go there, and my parents made up the remainder of the fees by working two jobs each. I think they thought they were giving me a head start in life, but as far as I'm concerned it was the worst thing they could have done.

From the start, I was terribly unhappy there. Because my parents didn't pay the entire school fees, I was immediately labelled one of the have-nots. All the other kids turned up at the start of term in Rolls-Royces with brand new luggage and hundreds of pounds in their tuck shop accounts, while I had my shabby old luggage and struggled by on just two shillings a week. I decided right there and then, watching the other children roll up and look down their noses at me, that I would make a success of my life and one day I'd have the best of everything.

I soon discovered that children have a very interesting habit of targeting any weakness you may appear to have. There were only two scholarship boys at the school – I was one and the other had to leave because he couldn't stand the verbal bullying. That's how bad it was. Over the ten years I was at that boarding school, I made no friends at all. I can honestly say I hated every minute of it and counted down the days until I could leave. To this day I have no idea why my parents didn't move me out of there. Maybe they thought it was character building. It wasn't. It was sheer misery, the worst experience imaginable.

The one thing the school did do for me was to make me determined no one would ever again be able to look down at me because of what I didn't have. From a very early age I started looking into ways of making money. My first big success was in dealing with rare coins.

At school I got into the habit of spending my pocket money on collecting coins. I quickly learned all the valuable dates and built up a sizeable collection. Then, in the early 1970s, there was a boom in the price of silver and any silver coins in circulation dated before 1947 became worth basically three times their face value. So a two-shilling piece would be worth six shillings. I saw a big opportunity. I was in my last two years at school and I already knew I wasn't going to go to university. All I was interested in was making money, so I started selling my coin collection and using the proceeds to buy more which I'd sell on again. I was basically trading in coins, and immediately I knew trading was what I wanted to do.

By the time I left the hated boarding school at 18, I'd amassed around £40,000 – a fortune in those days. But my relationship with my parents had never really recovered from them sending me to that school and keeping me there, even though I was so obviously unhappy. My mother died not long after I finished school, and my father couldn't really look me in the eye. We never managed to build up any sort of relationship after that – a shame when you think I was his only child. So I didn't go home. Instead I booked myself into a suite at the Grand Hotel in Birmingham. I used one of the rooms as an office and started trading in rare coins and bullion. I think my father was just flabbergasted. There was nothing he could do about it anyway. Every now and then he'd pop in to see if I was all right, but we didn't really have that much to do with each other.

It was funny because people used to come into the office and as I was so young, they'd ask, 'Where's your father?' They just assumed he must be running the business, not me. I loved it. I could see this was an opportunity to make a lot of money – and that's exactly what I did. I was a millionaire by the time I was 21. I used to drive Porsches and Rolls-Royces and drink the most expensive wines when I was 18 and 19. I'd moved into a five-bedroom house with a swimming pool before I was 21.

I could have stopped there. I had everything I wanted. I could have just stayed treading water, but something inside me wouldn't let me just sit back and coast. That's one of the things about successful people – they never lose their drive. I've known some very wealthy people in my life and they're all the same. It doesn't really matter if you've got £18million or £20million or £22million. That ten per cent up or down isn't going to change your lifestyle one iota. You've got a house that's worth £3million or £4million, you've got your cars, you've got money saved, you've got your pension and your kids are in private school. So what makes a man worth £20million want to go out and earn another £2million or £5million or £10million? It's a mystery, yet the super-rich are the most driven people I've ever met. The multi-millionaires work just as hard; they're just as careful, just as shrewd as anyone just starting out.

I think that once you lose that urge or that knack, that desire to go out and still want to succeed even though you've already made your millions, your empire will crumble. I'd made my money, but I wanted more. I wanted materialistic things. I wanted to be able to travel wherever I wanted, to have expensive cars, to go out and eat in the best restaurants. Perhaps because of growing up surrounded by people who were better off than me, no matter how much money I had it never seemed enough.

That's why, in 1981, I went to live in America to work as a commodities trader. You know in films when you see the people in the brightly coloured jackets waving their arms around? Well, that was me. Basically it's a sophisticated auction scheme where you're bidding on and offering products to other traders. The products I used to deal in were precious metals like gold, silver and platinum. I was trading on the exchange floor with my own money. Ridiculous amounts changed hands. On a volatile day I could make or lose a fortune.

I loved the work. It's the most exciting way of making money I can think of, and I was very successful, but it's stressful and it's lonely. When you're trading, you're not standing with other people who are trading in the same thing. You're standing in the trading pit for five hours a day, totally on your own, and it's very draining. I'd work 20 days in New York and then fly off to Los Angeles for ten days to recuperate. I had an apartment in Beverly Hills where I relaxed and led the Hollywood lifestyle with lots of friends. It was a perfect way to live.

It all came to a very sudden end one day in 1983, when immigration officials burst into the exchange floor looking for Mexicans working illegally. They came in while I had my back to the door so I didn't see them. When they realised I was English, they asked for my papers and green card, which was a problem because I didn't have either. I was given two weeks to produce them. I went to see a lawyer who said, 'You can either marry a nice American girl, or you can leave the country.' I left the country.

By this stage, I had a couple of million quid – easily enough to have sat on my laurels for a bit, but I'm too driven to do that. Back in Birmingham, I founded a company trading in precious metals, and that's when I ran into trouble. I was dealing in imported gold bars and at some point along the chain, the VAT hadn't been paid. I found myself being investigated as part of a multi-million-pound fraud case. While those investigations were underway, the VAT people uncovered an unrelated misdemeanour to which I pleaded guilty. The result was that I was sentenced to six months in prison while still awaiting the other trial.

The prison I went to was a local one in Sudbury, near Birmingham. I didn't mind it, to be honest. It was much better than boarding school – nicer people, better lifestyle and a much higher class of criminal. Generally speaking it was quite easy going. I came out in 1987, fighting fit and ready for my VAT trial, which I ended up winning. The problem was that defending myself at the trial had used up all my money. Customs and Excise officials had obtained injunctions freezing all my assets – my home, cars – they took all that and only released them as and when I got the bills from my legal defence team. Basically I got through the lot defending my case. You don't get the legal fees back, even if you've been acquitted.

So, in my early thirties, having made and lost a fortune, I found myself in the position of having to start all over again. But do you know what? I didn't really mind too much. I know that sounds funny, but I knew I was going to make it all back again. You've got to believe in yourself. You've got to have confidence, otherwise you have nothing.

I moved down south to the Thames Valley and went back into trading in a brokerage house. I stopped trading again on a day in 1992 – the day the chancellor put the interest rates up twice in one day. In that one day I made £14million. And guess what? It all went again. Bad trading, an excessive lifestyle, racehorses… It was amazing how quickly it disappeared. I'd got used to living really well. People say, 'How can you spend £75 on a bottle of wine?' But when you've made a million pounds that day, what do you care if the wine in the evening costs £75 or even £750? You lose sight of the value and meaning of money. I think that's how I managed to get through so much so quickly.

At the same time I started trading in investment rare coins. In the late 1980s and early 1990s I had a public company in London. Basically I was 20 years ahead of my time. Everything I was selling as investments then is now worth a lot but at that time the market went down. We were a very enthusiastic and quite aggressive company. We wanted to establish ourselves quickly, and we ended up making some untrue statements in advertisements in various magazines and brochures that we published. It wasn't long before I was back in trouble with the law, accused under the Company Act of making false claims.

The case dragged on for three long years before finally going to court in 1996. Originally I had the other directors in the company as co-defendants, but I ended up in the dock on my own as, due to a bureaucratic mix up, they weren't extradited from Canada. I managed to negotiate a plea-bargain deal with the judge – in return for pleading guilty I'd receive an 18-month sentence. But that judge ended up having a heart attack while watching the cricket, so instead of the 18 months I'd negotiated, I had to go to trial where I was found guilty of fraud and received a six-year sentence.

Six years is a long time. There's a huge difference between six months (my first sentence) and six years. On the way to prison in Hemel Hempstead I decided I would never make those sorts of mistakes ever again. And I haven't.

Some people do very well out of prison – think of Jonathan Aitken and Jeffrey Archer. You have to be a survivor. You can't let the bastards grind you down. While I was in prison I wrote a book about the fortune I'd made in a day and how I'd thrown it all away on having a good time. It was called *High Stakes: How I Blew £14 Million*. But I also hadn't told my father what had happened to me – by then he was a bit senile anyway – and he died while I was in prison. It was awful going to the funeral accompanied by a police officer. What little family I had left was totally hostile towards me – they felt I'd let my father down. It was a dreadful experience.

Being in prison forced me to rethink my attitude to money. Being around people who literally have nothing teaches you the value of things. I started saving while in prison, even though it was paltry sums – £5 or £10 a week. That was really the beginning of a whole new way of thinking for me. I'd always been a squanderer of money; in prison I became a saver.

I served three years of my six-year sentence, ending up in Ford Prison in West Sussex. When I got out in 1999 I had hardly any money, and I realised very quickly that it's almost impossible to rebuild a business in the UK after a lengthy prison sentence. You can't even open a bank account. I wasn't about to go and work for anyone else. I've never worked for anyone in my life. I think people who do that are fools. All they're doing is paying their mortgages. If I wanted to set myself up in business or trade, I knew I couldn't do it in the UK. Besides, I needed a fresh start – a clean bill of health, so to speak – so I started thinking about moving abroad. I was on parole for a year and not allowed to travel, but I started to plan where I would go.

The obvious choices for me were South Africa or Spain. I'd been to South Africa a few times and knew there were good business opportunities in the field I'm in, but the politics and the violence there worried me. So I opted for the Costa del Sol in Spain. I didn't know anyone there but I wanted to be somewhere with a ready-made English community where I could do what I was good at.

As soon as I was allowed to leave the country, I went to Spain, arriving with practically with nothing. But I never once entertained any self-doubt. Confidence is one of those things you either have or you don't. It's the same with trading. I have clients who've paid tens of thousands of pounds to have one-to-one tuition to learn how to trade. I go to see them and they've got £8million houses and loads of money in the bank, but they cannot trade. They know how to make money in any business, whether it's property or whatever, but they simply cannot trade. You can't teach anyone to trade. You can either do it or you can't. It's the same with confidence.

One day soon after I'd arrived in Spain I wandered into a bar to watch a horse race and the guy behind the bar asked me what I did. I said, 'I'm a trader,' and he said they were looking for someone to be the bar's bookie – to take bets on sporting events that were televised in the bar. I took the job and within six months I was running the bookmaking at eight different bars. It was a very successful business.

I was a bookmaker for my first few years in Spain. Then I entered a competition on the radio to see who could make the biggest return on an imaginary £100,000 within three weeks, using a trading platform. I ended up with £2.7million and a slot on the radio. I got a bit of a following and people started asking me if I could do that with real money, so I started trading with other people's money.

After losing a fortune twice some people would lose their nerve, but not me. You've got to have guts, ability, discipline, money management skills and, most of all, a willingness to take a risk. I've been in prison twice and I've experienced the worst life can throw at you and I know I can survive it. That puts me in a stronger position than most. People are frightened of going broke – which I've done. They're frightened of going to prison – which I've done. I don't have those sorts of fears. Many mega-successful people have gone broke at least once and some several times. You learn by your mistakes. In fact, the determination not to let that happen again is a real motivator.

In 2007 I had a near-death experience when a stomach ulcer burst. I had eight blood transfusions and am very lucky to be alive. I think now I've even overcome the fear of death. Nothing scares me now. Actually that's not entirely true. There is one thing that scares me – failure. I suppose in the end that's what motivates us all, isn't it? I'll never stop striving for more. True, you can only do so much with money. You can only drive one car at a time. You can only stay in one hotel room. But once you lose the desire to keep going, you're lost. I've known of billionaires who still get up at six in the morning to trade. You never let up.

I love playing poker. A couple of years ago I was in Puerto Banus and one of the other players was Victor Chandler, the multi-millionaire bookmaker. The bet level was 100 euros – small change to someone like him, but Victor played like granite. You'd have thought he was playing with his last 100 euros in the world.

'Why are you playing so carefully?' someone asked him. 'You can afford to lose 100 euros.'

His reply was, 'I take every bet as seriously as another, whether it's 10 euros or a thousand euros. I hate to lose anything. If you lose sight of that desire to win, that value you put on winning, the only way is down.'

That's my philosophy too. I'll only stop thinking about making money when I go to that big trading platform in the sky, and I'll never stop playing to win, no matter how big or small the stakes.

CHAPTER 8

ROSS WILLIAMS
WHAT HAVE YOU GOT TO LOSE?

In the short time since he hit on the idea of a dating website 'umbrella' application – which provides the infrastructure for thousands of smaller partner sites – Ross Williams has made a fortune. And as he met his girlfriend through one of his own sites, maybe the 30-year-old entrepreneur is proof that money can buy you love.

Up to the age of 14, I was a pretty middle-of-the-road child. All my school reports would say things like 'shy' or 'nice lad'. I didn't stand out in any way academically. I didn't excel at sports either, even though I'm six-foot three. I just kind of coasted along in the middle. All that changed when I joined the RAF cadets and learned to fly at weekends and evenings. At 14 I was flying a glider solo. At 17 I was flying a plane. At 18 I got my pilot's licence, just three months after my driving licence.

Suddenly I was the best at something. Better still, I was the best at something other kids thought was really cool – don't forget *Top Gun* – and it really changed something in me. When you're 18 and flying in the back of a Hawk jet through the Welsh valleys, it gives you confidence in yourself. Now, when I'm recruiting, that's what I look for in other people – that self-belief that comes from knowing you're the best at something. It doesn't matter what it is – you just have to excel.

I was born and raised in Ascot, which sounds posher than it actually was. I had a comfortable upbringing – my dad was a computer salesman who went on to become operations director of an IT company in Windsor. My mum started her own property rental company. Neither business was large scale. My dad was very much a salesman who owned 25 per cent of the company he worked for, while my mum's property company rented out about 20 houses. But I think having two self-employed parents, each running their own company, demystified the whole business world for me. I never saw it as something scary or risky. The first thing that stops most people starting up for themselves is fear. I never had that. To me, going into business for yourself was just something people did. My attitude was always: what have I got to lose?

My first foray into the business world came when, while still at school, I stumbled across a market stall in Bracknell selling three magazines for £1. Anyone could see that was a good deal, so I bought a dozen, took them to school and sold them to my classmates for £3 each. I did that for quite a few weeks until the teachers found out about it and put a stop to that particular sideline. Still, I'd made myself a few hundred pounds and, more importantly, got the selling bug.

In 1997, while studying psychology at the University of Plymouth, I started another sideline – designing and developing websites for small businesses. I'd helped out a bit at my dad's company and learned the basics of IT but hiring myself out as a designer still involved quite a lot of learning on the job. By the following year I was generating enough business to start a proper website design company, which I called Rawnet.

For the next five years, I slogged away at that company, going to meetings, chasing the next deal. I learned a huge amount, but it was hard work. In 2002 I took on my first employee, and for a month we worked together out of my parents' spare room before moving to an office in Bracknell. By staying small and growing the company very gradually, we managed to survive the dotcom crash and upscaled our operation to offices in Windsor. But still the big rewards eluded me.

Don't get me wrong, it was a good company – it still is – but initially I got a lot of basic things wrong. My biggest mistake was to make myself too much a part of the infrastructure of the company, so it was only valuable if I was there. The secret to expanding a company, I've learned the hard way, is to make sure it will still work even if you remove yourself from the equation. I didn't do that, which meant the company wasn't saleable. When all your assets are in your personnel, why would anyone buy the company if it means those personnel don't work there any more? Nowadays whenever I start up a business, I make it a policy to gradually phase myself out of it. I want to make sure that if I don't turn up for two months, the business will carry on running. That makes it a saleable commodity.

The other thing I learned from Rawnet was the importance of building a recurring revenue model into your business. For example, if you offer to build someone a website for £5,000, once that website is built you've got to go chasing after more business. Whereas if you offer to build it for £500 a month, it's a much better return. Once you've build it, it's revenue every month.

At the end of 2003, I decided to branch out and go into the dating industry. It was a boom area at the time plus, conveniently, I was single and needed a bit of a helping hand in that department. I'd been on a few dating sites (all in the name of research, obviously) and realised there were areas which could be vastly improved, particularly in regards to automatic rebilling after a subscription period was up. So I started contacting the sites' owners to offer Rawnet's services.

Meanwhile I was realising that while there was room in the marketplace for many dating sites, as people often sign up for several at once, most smaller ones were unable to compete with the marketing might of the two or three market-leaders. This made me start pondering the idea of setting up a centralised dating application that would provide all the infrastructure – the software, membership database, hosting, payment processing, billing and support system. This could then be accessed by unlimited smaller niche sites in a sort of franchise partnership system. The more we researched the idea, the more convinced I became that it could work. So we set up Global Personals, and soon afterwards launched Whitelabeldating.com and Singles365.com.

Of course, as director and token single, it was my duty to road-test the products. You wouldn't run a carvery if you don't eat meat, so why would I run a dating website if I hadn't used one? I signed up to our site and to competitors' sites to make sure they weren't offering anything that I wasn't offering my own customers. Now that I'm in a relationship, it seems crazy that I'd think nothing of driving two hours to meet someone for a date. Once I even went to New York for a first date. Happily, it was through my own site, Singles365, that I met my girlfriend. I wouldn't like to say that I used my position to influence her or anything, but I have to admit that messages from some of her other potential admirers might just have found themselves inadvertently deleted.

Right from the start the dating company almost ran itself. We bought a whole load of advertising on Google on our credit cards, moving the credit around from card to card until we recouped the money to pay off the original card and so on. As long as you know you're going to get that money back eventually, it's so simple.

By early 2007 that dating business was turning over hundreds of thousands a month, but I was still only spending three hours a week on it. It had a staff of six and ticked over quite nicely without me. The rest of my time was still eaten up with slogging away with Rawnet. Then late one Friday night, as I was leaving the office after a really stressful week, I had one of those moments of epiphany. Why was I spending so much time on a company that wasn't so profitable, instead of focusing on the one that was?

In September 2007, having moved up my number two up to take over at Rawnet, I relocated myself permanently to Global Personals. Our business model is so simple, and it's all consumer based. Suppose membership costs £20 a month. It might cost £20 in marketing to recruit that member, but after that it costs very little to look after them. Once you've grasped that, it's easy to start making money.

Since we started we've grown phenomenally quickly. We now operate about two thousand dating sites – if you Google 'dating' about 50 per cent of the sites that come up will be powered by us. We also work a lot with magazines that run their own dating sites using our infrastructure. I probably get about two or three wedding invites a month from people we've helped to find love, which is very gratifying.

The great thing about an internet business is it's very easy to expand internationally – you don't have to have a physical presence overseas. We've launched support for members in the US, Canada, Australia, New Zealand and South Africa. My aim is to carry on building the business up for another three to five years, then sell – by that point, on current projections, it should be worth around £60million. Then I'll put the money into another opportunity and repeat the pattern.

I'm a firm believer that you should never rest on your laurels, or try to hone a business until it's perfect. You have to see each business as a stepping-stone to the next – go into it looking at what you'll be able to sell it for and where the exit is. Keep setting goals, and when you reach them just set some more.

My first dream was to drive a TVR. When I got that, the goal moved to an Aston Martin, then it was a convertible Aston Martin and now I'm about to take delivery of the top-of-the-range DBS model. After that I'm going to be looking at a helicopter licence. It's all material stuff, I know, but it keeps me going. And when I've got everything I want, I'll use my skills for something other than money. I've got that competitive gene, so I'll always need to keep challenging myself but I'll transfer my efforts to some sort of charitable or non governmental organisation.

Once you reach a point where you've got enough to live on, it's too easy to sit back and get lazy, so it's healthy to keep setting goals. I not only write down my goals, I also make them public. True some people might take the mickey, or secretly want you to fail, but at least it gives you the best incentive to succeed. I used the same strategy when I was trying to lose weight. I put my weight online on a website for everyone to see so it became a matter of honour for me to slim down a bit.

When you're starting out, you have to make sacrifices. I was single for years because I put all my time into my company. But if you're prepared to do that, the rewards are immense. You don't have to start out with huge amounts of capital. The best businesses are the ones that start being run in your spare time and build up gradually. I hear people all the time saying, 'Oh, I haven't got the time to do that.' Of course they do. What they're actually saying is, 'It's not important enough for me to make time to do it.'

There's no secret to business. You just have to do it. When I look around at my own staff, I can see immediately that at least ten per cent of them should be working for themselves. The only thing stopping them is fear. Once you've overcome the fear, the only thing stopping you is not starting. Go for it!

CHAPTER 9

TONI COCOZZA
PROVING THEM
ALL WRONG

Written off at school because of her undiagnosed dyslexia, Toni Cocozza always felt she had a lot to prove. Now 45 and MD of top IT recruitment company DPConnect, she believes it's that chip on her shoulder that started her on the road to success

I'm a strong believer in possibilities. I think we should all look for the possibilities in life, rather than the barriers. When I was about 15, I went to see the careers officer at school. I had two dreams – to be an actress, because an actress can be anyone she wants to on any given day, or to be an air hostess, so I could travel the world. Looking up at the careers officer, I shyly outlined my ambitions, and I'll never forget the look of impatience on her face. 'Don't be ridiculous. You're far too short. Now, how about typing?' To this day, that scene influences the way I am and the way I run my recruitment company. In my philosophy, anything is possible, as long as you really want it. I would never discourage anyone from following a dream.

But that's not how things were when I was at school. I grew up in Catford and Beckenham in southeast London. My dad was a structural engineer and Mum was a housewife. I think we were working class, aspiring to middle class. You always think you've done all right, don't you, until you see what everyone else has got? I remember moving from our modest house in Catford to what seemed to me to be a mansion in Beckenham. But I was driving down there the other day and thought, What a sweet, tiny little house. At the time though, the garden seemed to me like a park.

It was quite an ordinary upbringing really. We were a loving, close knit Italian/Scottish family – lots of love there and lots of competitiveness between brothers and sisters. I'm the second of four children, with an older sister and a younger sister and brother. At school I struggled because I was dyslexic. I had big issues with the education system. I do think a lot of confidence problems I've had since have been about what happened to me at school: being taken aside for special reading lessons, the shame and embarrassment of not being able to read well, the humiliation of not doing well in exams.

In those days, nobody really knew anything about dyslexia, and it certainly wasn't diagnosed. In fact it wasn't until I was a mother myself that I realised why I'd struggled so hard. My youngest daughter was having problems at school and one of the teachers took me aside and said, 'We're sure your daughter is dyslexic.' I remember rushing back to the office really worried and sitting down at a computer to read up about it on the internet – but I couldn't even spell it! My business partner, Jan, had to come over and show me how to type it. We looked it up together, and all the things it was describing applied to me. I kept calling out different symptoms and people were looking at me and saying, 'Well, that's you.' And I said, 'Is it?'

That was quite hard for me, because it explained so much of what had happened to me when I was a child. I remember while I was waiting to be told that my daughter had got her official diagnosis of dyslexia, I received a phone call from Jan to say I'd been nominated for the title of Veuve Cliquot Businesswoman of the Year. I'd achieved this great honour, and yet I couldn't forget that at school I'd been made to feel so bad about myself. It was a bittersweet moment.

To this day, my father will pick up a note from me in the kitchen and complain that he can't read it. He just can't understand I will never be able to spell. My children now help me. My eldest daughter writes letters for me and checks my spelling. Now that it has a label, dyslexia is not such a horrible, shameful thing, but that's how I was made to feel for years. It affected my whole schooling. I was really good at verbal reasoning when I was 11, but I just couldn't do the written work, so I ended up going to the 'normal' school not the 'posh' one.

As time went on, my grades got increasingly worse. My claim to fame at school was that I was very good at challenging teachers and asking difficult questions. The other kids used to give me things in return for me asking one of my really clever questions which took up the whole lesson and meant we didn't have to do any work. I could talk intelligently and question and reason, but I couldn't get it on paper. My head goes too fast and my hands can't keep up. It's always been a hang up. Even now if I go to give a talk and leave my notes lying around I'm mortified in case people see how I write and spell.

I think the years of being stigmatised because of my writing led me to develop an 'I'll show them' attitude. It's also made me even more driven to achieve. Even now, I can't conceive of myself as a success. If people say, 'You're a success,' I always say, 'No, I'm not,' because I haven't yet got to where I want to be. I'm always striving towards something and I don't even really know what it is. I don't know if it's business. All I know is there's something missing that I'm still chasing after.

Over the years, you think it's the house, you think it's the money or the car but it's only when you achieve each of those things that you realise that all they are just badges to say to everyone, 'Look what I've made of myself.' Unfortunately those are the things other people use to measure success and it's only when you get there that you realise they don't mean anything. There's a lot more to life and to people and to doing good than what car you drive or how much you've got in the bank.

I realise now that a lot of what has motivated me has been ego and pride and a real desire to show the world that I wasn't the stupid little girl that school life had led me to believe I was. I don't know whether that will ever really leave me. After I saw the careers officer and was told to learn to type, I felt really deflated. I was only 15 and already I was being told what I couldn't do. Now I've got strong issues about how schools should motivate kids and sell them the idea of the workplace. Too often it's all about what you can't do, rather than all the possibilities of what you can do. We've done work over the years with the government and the Education Department to try to help change those attitudes.

To make matters worse, I didn't even pass the bloody typing tests, and I left school at 16 without qualifications. At the time I didn't want to work in an office. I wanted to do something different. I wanted to make an impact. I thought maybe I could be a female boxer. There was a real drive to make my mark on the world one way or another. My dad told me I was unrealistic. He said, 'There's no one who actually enjoys their job.' Well, at least now I can say he's wrong about that.

When I was leaving school I answered lots of ads in *The Lady*, thinking I'd be a nanny and travel, but I didn't get any offers. Then I decided to emigrate to Australia because my mum's family were there, but I didn't get enough points. So it was just a question of looking round locally for different jobs.

My first job was working in a pizza restaurant while I was still at school, which I enjoyed because it was working with people. Then after I left school, I worked in a holiday camp for the summer, making tea. But come September, I had to face the fact I needed a 'proper' job, so I started working for a same-day courier service. It was awful. All I was doing was ticking boxes. I lasted about six weeks. I'm an all or nothing person. As soon as my boss went out, I'd pull my chair out, put my feet up and go to sleep.

I didn't have a clue what job I wanted to do but the important thing was I wanted to enjoy it. I didn't want to be stuck in an office doing the same thing day in, day out. It wasn't about wanting to get rich, it was about being good at something. I wanted to be better than anyone else at something. That competitive edge has always been in me. I think a lot of it came from the low self-esteem that was instilled at school, and from sibling rivalry. I always felt like the underdog so I had to try a lot harder than anyone else.

Even though I run a successful company, there are still traces of that low self-worth. Even now I'll get up on stage to give a talk and give it this big attitude and then I'll come off and say, 'Do you think they liked me?' We were invited to speak at a conference a little while ago and I was so nervous. I was in the ladies beforehand and I turned to Jan and said, 'What would you think of me if I went home now?'

Along with the low self-esteem comes a real dread of letting anyone down. Even now, while the markets are diving and I'm going through a divorce, I'd never think about packing it in or even taking a break, because I'm determined not to let anyone down. I could never give up because there are so many people depending on me.

After I walked out of the courier company, I went to work for British Rail in the lithograph department. That was quite different. I had a thing about working in a man's industry – again I think I was trying to prove a point, that I wasn't this nice little Catholic girl who was a complete pushover. I was one of very few women they'd ever had working there. I was running the great big machines that produce timetables and posters. I enjoyed it in a weird way, but I ended up getting really bad rashes on my hands, so I had to give it up.

It was about 1980 when I saw a job ad for a recruitment consultant. It was a high-street operation where people literally walked in off the street to look for jobs. I didn't even know what a recruitment agency did but when I went for the interview I was hooked. It seemed so glamorous because instead of being stuck in an office, you were working with people. I'd always said to myself I couldn't work a 9–5. I've got such a low boredom threshold that I need to have lots of different things going on all the time. This job involved talking to lots of different types of people about different vacancies and working with large corporate clients who were looking for personnel. It was a whole new world.

It really was a case of learning on the job. One of my first interviewees was a mortician. I didn't have a clue what that was, but I knew I couldn't let on so I just kept asking him questions and bit by bit I realised what he'd meant. It was interesting, dealing with clients, getting to know about recruitment. It gelled with me because of my genuine interest in people. My boss was a lady who was quite entrepreneurial. I did well with her and was there for about two years. Then the recruitment market started failing and the business had to close, which was a real shame.

After that, I went into publishing and worked for Link House. I was still only about 20 or 21 and I was the only female advertising rep on their car magazine. I noticed a couple of managers who really got my back up because they'd come in and put their feet up and bark orders at people. That really helped to form my philosophy of how not to manage people.

While I was there, a woman set up as a psychic near the office and quite a few people from work went to see her. They'd come back saying she'd described me to a tee. In the end I got really fed up and rang her up and said, 'Who is this?' and she said, 'It's ME!' It turned out to be the woman who'd run the recruitment office I'd worked for! I kept in touch with her after that and when she went on to get a job in IT recruitment, she rang me and said, 'You've got to come and work here.' So I did.

The IT field was completely different from my previous recruitment job – so much more professional. When I was working for the high street company, you'd place a secretary and she'd come back in at lunchtime on her first day and say, 'I didn't like it.' IT, on the other hand, was a serious profession. We were dealing with mostly highly technical men, and learning about technology.

I worked there eight and a half years, working my way up through the ranks to sales director. I loved it and I made a lot of money. I remember being about 25 and thinking, I'm driving a Mercedes and I'm earning more than the prime minister of England. I'd sit at big board tables in the top banks. We'd do all our work before we employ someone. I'd get these top-name clients approaching us about employment and I'd say, 'Well, before I place anyone with you, I want to know why you'd make a good employer. I want to sit in on your meetings and meet your staff.' I'd make a real effort to understand the company – the spirit, the ethos.

When the recession of the late-1980s was looming I was told to lay off some of my team, which really upset me. The worst point came when someone came to see me and said they were about to take out a loan so their daughter could go back to university but before they did, they wanted to make sure their job was secure at least for three months. I said yes. Then I was told to let them go.

I went on half salary a few times to show solidarity to the staff. Then, as the recession hit, I found out I was pregnant and suddenly my clients started to be taken away from me. My integrity was being compromised, so I left.

I decided that after the baby was born, I'd set up my own recruitment company. It sounded so easy but when I went to see the bank manager, he told me I couldn't open a business account without headed notepaper. But I couldn't get headed notepaper without the name of the company – and to register a company I needed an account. It was so confusing. You couldn't get a bank account because you hadn't been trading and you couldn't get a telephone line because you hadn't been trading. Plus they gave me a great big pack talking about business plans and marketing plans and full of so many forms it made my head hurt just thinking about them. So when my husband, who ran a plumbing firm, offered me a tiny office above the firm's garage, and said I could use their phones and print my own headed notepaper off their printer, I jumped at it.

After my daughter was born in February 1990, I set up my company with zero finance behind me. In a sense, my naïvete and my innocence towards business actually helped, because without them I don't think I'd ever have had the nerve to get started. When I picked up that initial business pack from the bank, I thought, Forget that – I'm not going to borrow money from them. I decided I'd rather ask for a six-month mortgage break and provide my own funding than be forced to attempt to fill in all those forms and forecasts. Instead of getting bogged down in projections and looking at all the things that could go wrong, I tried to focus on the possibilities. I never had a proper business plan. I never had a proper strategy. I made it all up as I went along.

Even today, though we're so much more advanced, when it comes to putting a plan down on paper, I just can't do it. All I can see is a company here, an opportunity there, and if that doesn't work we'll do this or this. I'm very reactive. I try something and if it's not working out, I'll try something else. Planning something and sticking to those rules and following it through – well, that's just not the way I'm made.

That's why the team who work with me are so important – they have to give me that back up and structure.

Part of me thinks it was a good thing that I didn't do too much advance planning. I think people can spend too much time doing the research and not enough time actually doing the business. My advice to people starting out is always just go out there and start. Find out who your clients are. What can you do for them? Worry about the logo and the paperwork afterwards. If someone's setting up a business I love to help them. But sometimes they get so bogged down in the analytical data and background market research that not one of them is actually picking up a phone and making money.

That first office above the garage was a really humble start. Having had the big team, the company car, the plush office it was a real shock suddenly to be back in tracksuits with no furniture. Luckily, my husband spurred me on by challenging me. 'OK, you're always so quick to point out what other people are doing wrong, let's see how you do.' I wanted to prove to myself that I could do this. My whole life and attitude changed after having the baby. I wanted to be in control of my own destiny. I wanted to see if I was capable of doing it. I knew I couldn't go back and do what I had been doing and working the same hours with a new baby in tow. I know now it was a very brave decision, but still I don't see myself as a risk-taker. I see myself as someone who takes very calculated risks.

I started work in October 1990. That first year was really

tough. It was like starting at the bottom again, ringing around finding clients. My ego took a bit of a knock. I was ringing people and saying, 'Do you remember me? I worked with you a few years ago,' and they weren't bothering to return my calls. I'd also picked the worst time in the world – the recession had hit and I was trying to get clients that everyone else was after. And I was doing it with no facilities. It was a case of: 'I can't send you a contract because I can't type and I can't get a typewriter yet because the chairs aren't coming until Thursday.' I was literally sitting on the carpet in this tiny office. Even when I got a desk, there was no room, so when you got up to go, you had to shift all the furniture round just to open the door.

Looking back, it was exciting. It was fun. It could be great. But it was undeniably tough. The office was in Beckenham, near my parents' home, so I was lucky with childcare, but I still had to try to drum up the business.

Eventually I got some big clients, like Barclays. I got those mostly through helping people out when they were on hard times. During the recession a lot of people lost their jobs. All the new vacancies were advertised in trade magazines, but if you weren't employed by a company, you couldn't get one. So when I found out my clients had lost their jobs I rang them up and offered to photocopy my copy of the magazine and send it to them so they could apply for jobs. People remember things like that. These were managers and middle managers who had lost their jobs and suddenly found that the young recruitment agents who had been licking their toes a few weeks earlier, now wouldn't even ring them back. It was humiliating.

I'd work with these managers because I genuinely liked them and I wanted to work with them long-term. So when they got back on their feet, they picked me as their recruitment consultant. I've had a lot of clients who've started off in junior positions and ended up as senior managers, and they've come back to me time and time again when they wanted to recruit staff. So many times I've had people who'd hit hard times say to me, 'Toni, you're the only one who'll take my call.' So when they started recruiting again, I was in there.

As I gradually got busier and busier, I needed a secretary. I couldn't type and I couldn't keep getting my father-in-law to do it for me, so I went to one of the jobseeker schemes to help women return to work after having a baby. The employer had to pay £50 a week – which was the same as a woman would have got on benefits – and then she'd get an extra £10 on top of that. At first I thought it was exploiting them, but then I thought, No, it's giving them valuable experience. Plus I couldn't afford anything else.

I got sent a wonderful lady who had two small children and had been out of the workplace for ages. I loved and respected her because she worked from 9 to 5.30 and all she got was an extra £10 on top of what she'd have got for staying at home. That's my sort of person. That's the sort of person who says, 'I'm not going to look at what my lot is today. I'm going to look ahead to see what this could do for my life.' She did very well. One of my biggest Cilla Black moments was when I bought her one of those big Christmas socks and I filled it with cash, because we'd been doing quite well. She'd really helped me and we'd shared in it together.

The next member of staff was a girl I found from the Youth Training Scheme. I couldn't afford to employ anyone with experience, and anyway they'd only have told me all the reasons why I shouldn't be doing this or that. So I took on this YTS girl and she came in and was brilliant. She's now been with me 17 years and is one of my directors. She's been top saleswoman every single year. She's just absolutely amazing. She's so committed. I find it bizarre that I go home to my lovely house and my kids at private school, and even though it's her hard work that has helped make all that possible, she still leaves the office every day and says, 'Thank you.' She's unbelievable. What a work ethic! That's what this business has been built on.

We stayed in the office above the garage until we had a turnover of about £60,000. By that time there were three of us there – a secretary, myself and another member of staff. I was pregnant with my second child and we all had to swap desks because I couldn't physically get out of the door, so we moved to a bigger office above a record shop in Bromley. That gave us room for expansion, so we took another couple of people on.

For the first six months of the business, I didn't take a salary, and after that I only took a small amount. Everything else was put back into the company, because I was ignorant of how the money side of things worked. I didn't know you could go to a bank and say, 'Here are my accounts. Can you lend me some money?' Probably just as well really. We just paid for everything ourselves.

We were very old fashioned. I used to run round to my parents' house on a Sunday and do all my accounts myself, but I was never very good at the technical side. I'd be doing my Lotus spreadsheets and yell, 'I've lost £50,000!' and my mum would be really panicked. Then a few minutes later I'd find it had fallen into the wrong column or something. Before she died, my mum said, 'If that business isn't the death of you, it'll be the death of us.' My business ethos was that we were OK as long as we could continue trading and have enough to cover salaries for the next six months, plus a little bit put by for tax and a little for emergencies. Then if we secured a big deal, that'd buy us another month. It was all very short term.

I was always really excited whenever we moved offices, because obviously we were moving up one, always improving. We had a thing for years about when we would become a real company, and I suppose I didn't think we'd be a 'real company' until we owned our own offices, instead of sharing someone else's space or renting offices from a third party. Over the years I've said that to people and I can tell they've thought I'm mad. You can see them thinking, Blimey, she's turning over £24million and making a load of profit and she still doesn't think she's a real company!

Last December we finally got our own office block in

Bromley. You can't miss it – it's got so many flags outside it screaming, 'Whoo hoo – here we are!' So I suppose we are finally a bona fide company, and I should pat myself on the back. But in my head there's always more to do, always more opportunities. I'll never think, Right, we've made enough money now – simply because I don't really understand the financial side of things, even now.

There was a time when we had a new accountant, and I just got the papers out and said, 'Just tell me which line I should be looking at.' I think he was a bit shocked. Another time, after we'd been going six or seven years, we had the accounts done and the accountant said to me, 'Toni – you might have to sit down for this. You've turned over £3million, with £250,000 in profit.' I didn't even know what turnover was, so I said, 'Is that good?'

The next year we turned over £7million with £1million profit. The accountant chap said, 'Toni – you've made a million pounds this year.' I said, 'Does that mean...?' and he went, 'Yep, you're a millionaire.'

But that doesn't mean I'm great with money. We went through a phase where I employed lots of senior directors because I thought they'd have the experience and qualifications. It just didn't work. We employed one guy at great expense to tell us where we could save money. He spent ages and came up with two things.

1 Reduce the amount we put away for bad debts. Well, hello? Firstly this was only on-paper money and

didn't actually exist. Secondly, if we're worried about the way the market is going, why on earth would we reduce our cover for bad debt? I don't think so.

2 Not to let anyone have hot chocolate. He said we were too generous with tea and coffee. And as we spent a fortune on polystyrene cups, he advised us to think about putting names on these cups and giving them one cup each day.

We were paying this guy £100,000 a year. I remember thinking, Did he really have to go to school and college just to learn that?

One time our accountant actually had to tell me to start taking out more money. I couldn't believe it. My husband and I bought a new house, but we still took out a mortgage so that I could carry on ploughing money back into the company. I told my husband: 'If it all goes wrong and the house gets taken away, that can be our holiday – going round nice places and looking at what our lifestyle used to be like.' To this day, I can't conceive of how much money we've got. Unless I go to the cashpoint and see a balance of £1million in my personal account, I won't feel like a millionaire, which is probably what keeps me going.

Yes, there have been bad times along the way. People have let me down. I have high expectations and it hurts me when people don't live up to them. I've had times when I've felt like the loneliest person in the world. And I've had all the work-life balance issues and the guilt about not being there for my kids. Jan and I joke about our kids turning up to school for 'own clothes day' in their uniforms, or us being pulled aside half way through term to ask if it might be possible for them to have a PE kit like all the other children.

But in some ways, being female has helped me in business. The majority of our competitors who own businesses are male and I think I get away with things a man maybe wouldn't. I just go into places and say, 'Do you mind if I come in and see how your business works?' People are usually lovely if you ask. There's this whole ethos of 'I'm not telling you my secrets' but if you get past that you can really help each other out.

In fact if I had to pinpoint my proudest achievement in business, it would be been allowing people to be better than they think they are. I enable them to get the best out of themselves, and that gives me a huge kick. When I recruit staff, I'm looking for the chip, that hang-up that gives them something to prove, because that to me means they'll be motivated. So a lot of my initial staff were mums getting back to work or single mothers or young guys without proper qualifications. We had such a cross-section. We had really posh people who were here because Daddy's got so much money and they want to show Daddy they can do it without his help, and we'd have people with nothing. It's always been a mixture. It's about understanding human beings and about looking out into an office and saying, 'Why does that person work here? What are they trying to get out of it?' If you can understand that, you're going to get more from them.

I remember one woman came to an interview years ago and she said it was the first company where she'd ever been asked, 'Yes, but what do *you* want to do? True, you could easily do this, this and this, but what is it you *really* want?' That way of thinking has really helped shape my company. It's all very well for people to do what I ask them to do but if they're doing what *they* really want to do, I'm going to get so much more out of them.

Yes, we've got it wrong many a time. But I think if you bear in mind that your staff are the people that keep your company afloat, you'll always do right by them. Yes, you have to be the boss and you have to make the tough decisions, but you also have to let those people know that without them there is no business. I always say that in my company you work your way down – because the people who are traditionally at the 'bottom' of a company structure are actually the most important. It's a different style of management. It's about empowering by giving opportunities.

I'm always honest to my staff. I used to work for this chap and he'd call in a member of staff and tell them how great they were, and then as soon they'd gone he'd say, 'No, he's no good. Give him a week's notice.' And I used to think, Why not be honest with him? Why don't you sit with him and say, 'I appreciate your opinion, but here this is what works best, and if you don't do X it's not going to work'? At least that gives him the chance to get things right.

As a manager I think I can be very loving and motivational, but I can also be very hard. A lot of people are shocked. I've had people come in on a four-month probation and they're really taken aback when I sit down with them after a month and say, 'These are the reasons I think you might fail.' They say, 'So you want me to leave then?' And I say, 'No, hang on a minute – you've still got three months. I just wanted to tell you now so you have a chance to do something about it.' At the end of the day, those people are working here for themselves, their families and their lives. And if I treat them correctly they're also working for me and my family.

In some businesses I'm shocked when I walk in and see how they treat their staff. People might have different paypackets, different capabilities, but that doesn't make them a better or worse human being. There should be decency and honesty amongst people – yes, even in a business environment. I can be tough sometimes, but I love the fact that someone could walk into the office and not know if I was the cleaner or the managing director. I love that.

I've been running a successful business for years now but I'm learning things all the time – both professionally and personally. I'm finally dealing with the low self-esteem issues and learning to feel comfortable and tranquil with myself. But I still don't know what motivates me to keep going, or what I'm aiming to achieve. I know it's not about money, even though I've loved being able to use my money to help people. True, I used to have a bad day in the office and then drive home to my beautiful house in the country and see my children running around and the dog and the whole fairytale lifestyle and think, That's what I do it for. But nowadays I'm looking for something even more than that. I still don't know what it is that's going to make me feel 'Yes, I've done it!' I don't think I'll know until I get there.

Sometimes I think – morbid, I know – about my own funeral and wonder, How much good did I do in my life? How many other people's lives have been made different because of me? I don't just mean money and cars and things. I want to leave the planet having done something worthwhile. I've always given money to charity. People say, 'You can't give that bloke £50,' but the truth is that me giving him £50 is the same as a person on a low income giving 5p, and it's going to make such a big difference to him. I'm nothing special but I do feel fortunate I can do that.

Nowadays I try to give time as well as money. There's a lot I'd like to do for young kids – things to do with education and schooling. At one stage I was going to do the *Secret Millionaire* programme and live with young girls who'd got pregnant and needed a helping hand to get back to work, and get their self-esteem back. In the end I pulled out because of family issues, but that's the kind of thing I'd have loved to do.

Don't get me wrong: I love running a business, and I love

the fact that I've been able to help people achieve their potential, but that isn't the mark I want to make on the world. I don't know what it is, but I'll just keep going until I find it.

CHAPTER 10

STEFAN WISSENBACH
PASSION AND BELIEF

Having built and sold four businesses, Stefan Wissenbach, 40, is now CEO of The Wissenbach Group, which provides financial advice to high net worth individuals. He has developed the concept of the Magic Number – the amount of money that enables every individual to achieve financial independence so they can enjoy their desired lifestyle

At the age of 16, five months into my A level course, I decided I wanted to leave school. My mum was a head teacher and believed passionately in the value of studying for as long as possible, but I was desperate to get out there and start earning money. She sat me down on the edge of my bed and I vividly remember her sternly conceding the point with a firm ultimatum: 'I'll allow you to leave school, but only if you promise me that by the time your age group is leaving university, you'll be ahead of them on the career ladder. You have to have made use of this head start.'

Five years later, when my contemporaries were graduating, I was responsible for graduate recruitment at the company I worked for. It was my responsibility to employ the university leavers – the very people who'd been my contemporaries at school. The process of establishing a clear, measurable objective and then going on to benchmark myself against it instilled in me a lifelong habit of setting goals – and then formulating a plan of action that would allow me to meet them.

Even before then, my mum was a huge influence on me because she brought my younger sister and me up more or less single-handedly. She'd met my father when they were both working in Switzerland; they moved to England when I was three, but they'd split up by the time I was nine. Consequently, things were really tight financially. We lived in a cramped two-bedroom flat in Aylesbury, and when my sister and I grew too old to share a room comfortably, my mum chose to sleep on a sofa bed in the living room so we each had our own space.

But my mum always believed absolutely that we could achieve big things and that sense of conviction has been one of the great guiding forces of my life. She was always striving to move forwards, for us and for herself. At night she studied for an Open University degree, became a teacher, and eventually worked her way up to the position of head. This considerable achievement was constantly kept on track by her firm belief that 'You should always be the best you can be.' So when I was nine, the television was thrown out and we were encouraged to improve our minds through reading. At the time I thought this desperately unfair and railed against it, but with the benefit of adult hindsight, I appreciate what she was trying to do. A coach recently told me, 'Remember, when you're watching TV, you're watching someone else make their fortune.' I think that's absolutely true. It's often dead time.

I have always been very ambitious, but I don't know if that attribute originated from having a limited number of material possessions as a child. I was accepted into a good school – Aylesbury Grammar – but despite achieving nine O levels, I lost focus after that and wanted to leave. When my mum saw how passionate I was about getting a job, she let me quit school – but not without extracting that promise first!

Sixteen sounds very young, but looking back I think I was probably quite mature for my age. From the age of ten I'd been the man of the house, so I think that probably helped me grow up a bit quicker than I might otherwise have done. And as I mentioned, my mother had instilled in me this unshakeable belief that everything would work out in the way I had planned. It sounds like a cliché now to say, 'What the mind can believe, it can achieve,' but it's true. Belief brings achievement.

So in 1984 I left school and went to the careers office in Aylesbury. At that point they used a system whereby they asked you loads of questions, then fed your answers into a computer the size of a transit van and it spat out a piece of paper telling you what job you'd be good at. Mine said I should do something in finance or banking.

As a result I joined one of the two financial services companies in Aylesbury – Target Life, where I was lucky enough to have a manager who took me under his wing and became a mentor to me. He gave me lots of sound advice, such as to show commitment by getting in early and leaving late. When I started arriving early, I noticed that the only cars in the car park were the Jaguars belonging to the directors. So I decided to come in even earlier, so I was there before they arrived. That way I came to their attention (although you could argue that they couldn't very well ignore me when I was the only person in a deserted office). One board director in particular would chat to me on his way in. He started enquiring about me, namechecking me in meetings and it wasn't long before I was promoted.

It didn't take me long to notice that every so often certain other guys would turn up for meetings in the office. They all drove Ferraris and Aston Martins, but only stayed an hour or two and then left again. 'Who are they?' I asked, awestruck. 'They're the financial advisors who sell all the products we deal with,' I was told. I realised there and then I was in the wrong job.

Through hard work and that demonstration of commitment, I got fast-tracked through the company until I was running my own department. Within five years, I was responsible for employing the new graduate intake from university and more importantly, I had fulfilled the all-important promise to my mother. After that I took a job in Birmingham working for another branch of Target Life, the National Financial Management Corporation. I felt fairly pleased with my career progress, but looking back, I still had a wealth of experience to acquire.

While I was at Aylesbury I'd carried on living at home,

but when I was offered the job in Birmingham I decided to buy a place of my own there. I didn't know anything about the city, but I rang an estate agent who offered to show me a flat in a place called Winson Green. 'That sounds nice – green and leafy,' I thought, not knowing that it was actually one of the roughest areas in the region and right next to a prison. The agent picked me up at the station and drove me to the flat, perhaps taking a route that avoided all the blackspots. I took a look at the flat, thought it looked adequate and agreed to buy it for £21,000. It was only when I moved in that I realised just how horrible it was. That was in 1988 and it wasn't until 2001 that I was able to sell it – and even then I only got what I'd paid for it 13 years before. So I was far from infallible.

After a few years in Birmingham, my first mentor from Target Life headhunted me to work for another financial services company based in Milton Keynes, where I ran the New Business and the Customer Services departments, among others. In the most basic terms I was doing well – I was assigned a company car and participating in a rewarding bonus scheme. But I knew it wasn't what I wanted to do long-term – it wasn't where my passion lay. I'd already come to the conclusion that my career strategy should centre around working at something until it had run its course and then move on – not stagnate. I also knew I wanted the material things that I'd lacked in my early life – to drive a nice car, live in a nice house. By this stage my wife Diana and I were living in a terraced house in

Harborne, on the outskirts of Birmingham. It was definitely a step up from Winson Green, but a long way from the huge, rambling home of my dreams.

So I decided to start my own financial advisory business. This meant giving up the security of my salaried job, but thankfully my wife supported me completely. 'What's the worst that could happen?' we'd ask ourselves. 'That we have to sell the house and buy a Harley Davidson and go off and find bar work? That's not so bad.'

The day I left I had to give my company car back, so I bought an old Jeep from one of the staff to travel home in. On the way home I had an accident on the M40 and wrote off the Jeep. So, my first day with a new business, and I had no car and very little money! Thankfully, this troubled start wasn't a sign of things to come.

I was fortunate enough to find another mentor, an experienced financial advisor who helped me build the business to a point where it was time to recruit employees. The whole team – Diana, myself and two members of staff – started off working from our dining room table.

I've always subscribed to the school of thought that the best business models cater to a very specific need, so my business model was quite simple – to pick a niche, specialise in a particular area and make it work. I focused on people working in the IT sector, who were often employed on fixed contracts and needed someone to manage their financial affairs. We got to know everything about this group of people and really addressed their needs, building our reputation on honesty, integrity and 'best of breed' services delivered efficiently. In any business, if you provide something of value, if you're honest and you act with integrity, you'll thrive. I'd only ever recommend to clients something I'd do myself if I were in their shoes. This philosophy paid off, the company grew rapidly and before long we'd moved to offices in the Birmingham Stock Exchange.

Before long I saw another opportunity, and in 1994 I branched out into IT recruitment. That business really took off very quickly until it was turning over more than £5million. I was on a roll – working four days a week and taking 12 weeks holiday, but still running a business that was getting real results.

Then the dotcom bubble burst. Over a 12-week period, the recruitment company went from making £60k–£70k profits a month to a £50k loss per month. More than 80 per cent of our client base was laid off. The recruitment company was no longer making the margins it needed, because these relied on clients being in work, and the financial services business dropped hugely in profit because the majority of its clients were no longer in jobs. In 2000 I had to put the recruitment business into liquidation and eventually I sold my financial services business too.

That was a really painful time for me. There were many emotional evenings at home when Diana and I would think, What on earth have we done? We had three children by this stage and, to complicate matters further, we'd bought a big country house the previous year and embarked on an ambitious programme of renovations. But I couldn't allow it to affect my confidence. After all, no one had predicted the dotcom bubble bursting. Instead I tried to take something from what had happened. I wrote a document called *Lessons Learned*. I've still got it, all these years later. In it I listed the mistakes I'd made – like overexposure to one market and not cutting costs soon enough. I wouldn't make those mistakes again.

Keeping on only 12 clients from my financial services business, I re-branded the company and focused on a different niche that had a far broader client base – high net worth. We set up business from offices in the grounds of our house and I remortgaged the property and used up all my savings to pay for staff wages. Gradually we built ourselves up again from scratch.

During this time I started going to Chicago to see a coach to help me develop my business and personal strengths – someone with an independent perspective who could help me move forward. Seeing a coach every three months helped me to keep my focus sharp and forced me to be more disciplined. Through coaching I recognised my strengths in business, which are understanding situations and identifying opportunities. I'm also very good at starting things and visualising a successful outcome, but not so good at carrying them through to a conclusion. So I now make sure I surround myself with a team of people who can complement my strengths. We put all our staff through a process that identifies their skills and make sure we put them in roles that match those skills. This approach has been successful and has enabled me to develop a strong core business, as well as go on to grow and sell four other companies.

Our new business strategy saw us bring in clients through recommendation, marketing to high net worth individuals and inviting them to seminars. We built a really robust business model to meet the needs of our target clients, addressing their frustrations and helping them to capitalise on their opportunities and utilise their strengths. We also developed the concept of the Magic Number – the amount of accumulated wealth an individual needs to be in a position of financial independence, where they can choose whether or not to work. People tend to pluck sums out of the air but we work it out for them based on a raft of detailed questions about where they want to live, how they want to spend their time, where they want to travel. We cost it out over a lifetime and work backwards until we arrive at how much they need each year. Once you arrive at that figure, people find they have only one of two problems – not enough money or too much! Knowing your magic number enables you to make really smart financial decisions.

It's so easy to overestimate how much you need. People usually say, 'I want £100million.' I know that was my end goal at one time. But when I really thought about it I realised it wasn't about the money, it was about the lifestyle. What I wanted above everything was a lifestyle where I worked hard but had the free time to enjoy what I worked for and spend time with my family. I realise now that from a lifestyle perspective, it doesn't really make a difference if your net worth is £50million or £100million. There are only so many meals you can eat, only so many houses you can live in.

Mind you, coming from a humble background, I do appreciate the things money can buy and the way I'm able to live. I do a daily gratitude focus where I concentrate on what's good in my life, which helps me maintain clarity and motivation. I also carry around a piece of paper that has all my goals written on it. First there's the long-range vision – to be happy, healthy, wealthy and living a focused and fulfilled life. Then I've broken that down into individual key goals, then I've set myself three-year targets which will lead me there, then one year, then 40 days and so on.

That doesn't mean I'm not flexible. You have to be open to opportunities and seize them as they come along, which means I'm constantly adapting my plans. But writing things down does keep you focused. I always remind myself of that 1953 study of the Yale graduating class where, 20 years later, the three per cent who actually wrote down their goals were found to be worth more than the other 97 per cent put together. If you've always got your goals in mind, you know where you're heading and opportunities will come your way. It's the same message in books like *The Secret* and *Think and Grow Rich*. People who can visualise and believe in the future – and connect with where they want to get to – attract circumstances that help them get there. Successful people have the ability to visualise.

The other qualities successful people share are belief and passion. You have to have belief in your ability to achieve. If you believe you're destined for a better future, you'll keep going, no matter how many setbacks you face. It's essential that your belief system doesn't crumble when you hit bad times. You have to turn it around and see those times as learning experiences, rather than failures. At my seminars in the US, some clients arrive in their private jets and one of the first things they ask me is, 'How many failures have you had?' It's a different mindset there – if you haven't failed, you haven't risked and more importantly, you haven't learned. In the UK, if you've failed, you're a failure. I think that as long as you have belief, you can use failure to your advantage.

But belief on its own isn't enough – you have to have passion too. You have to be passionate about what you do, otherwise you're going to fall on the first or second or third hurdle. Can passion be learned? That's the million-dollar question. If I'm ever working with someone who hasn't got that fire in the eyes, I can tell it's not going to work. You have to get turned on by what you get out of bed to do every morning, or you won't have the conviction to carry you through when things get rough.

I have a great life now. I work a four-day week and take long holidays. I spend a lot of time with my family and, increasingly, on charitable work – we are raising funds to build an eye hospital in Nepal. Sure, having grown up in a poor household I appreciate things like travelling around in a luxury car with a driver, or living in a nice house, but that's not what motivates me to keep getting up every day. If there's one thing I've learned it's this: life is not about money – it's about life.

CHAPTER 11

HAROLD TILLMAN
STYLE AND FLAIR

Number 244 in the 2008 Sunday Times Rich List,
Harold Tillman is estimated to be worth £365million.
But the head of fashion giant Jaeger and chairman of
the British Fashion Council has overcome more than
his share of obstacles along the way.

A couple years ago, I was at our Jaeger annual conference, where we give out awards to managers who've performed very well. I remember a staff member I'd never met before, gripping my arm and saying, 'Mr Tillman, thank you so much for saving the company.' Those words meant more to me than a million pounds. To know I've made a positive difference to people's lives makes everything worthwhile, and it's doubly precious because just 15 years earlier I'd been all but written off.

I remember opening a newspaper in those dark days and seeing myself referred to as 'threadbare Harold Tillman'. It was 1990 and up to that point I'd been the golden boy. I'd walked on water. Suddenly, with the closure of Honorbilt, the company I'd taken over a few years earlier, it was gone. All over. Today I'm back and Jaeger, the then-ailing company I took over in 2003, goes from strength to strength, but it's still painful to recall that period. But when you're down, you just have to get back up again and claw your way back. You have to work doubly hard.

I'm a very tenacious person. I get that from my father. Both my parents were incredibly hard working. My father was a tailor and my mother a milliner. My father was originally from Leeds, but I was born in London and we lived in a flat above a shop in south London before moving on to Streatham. As an only child I was very close to my parents and naturally became engrossed in their world – the clothing business. My dad had a clothing factory in Elephant and Castle where they made suits. Even as a teenager in the 1950s I had my clothes specially made for me.

My parents had a lot of style. Whatever they had, it had to be the best even if they had to save and save for it. Everything had to be good quality. That's something I learned at a very young age. But even though I loved the fashion world, my parents wanted me to be an accountant. My father was often unwell and I used to help out by doing the books for him, so I had already acquired some experience. Dutiful son that I was, I didn't want to disappoint them, so when I left school I studied accountancy – and hated it. It was so boring and so far from where my interests lay, so I took an entrance exam for the London College of Fashion. Being accepted on the course was like a ticket into a new life. I studied there for two years, one of very few male students, and it instilled in me a passion for learning about fashion and design that has never gone away.

After graduating, I went to work as an apprentice for one of my father's customers who had a company called Lincroft Clothing in Great Portland Street. I begged to be allowed to create my own clothes and ended up designing hipsters, which sold really well. It was the Swinging Sixties: I took my designs to Carnaby Street and they ended up making more money than the rest of the business put together. Three years after joining I got a loan and bought the company from the owners.

Being young, I understood the culture of the time. I knew about marketing and publicity. I got George Best, one of the coolest figures around, to promote the clothes. In those days I suffered from a kind of naïve tenacity. If I went to see a customer who wasn't interested, I would just keep going back to them, almost out of one door and back in through the next. I was so desperate to persuade them that we were good. I also had a good eye for spotting other young talent and got a young Paul Smith in to work for me.

The business succeeded very quickly. Partly because of my accountancy background and partly because of what I'd seen happen to the business of a friend's father, I decided that going public was the way forward. In 1969, at the age of 24, I became the youngest person ever to float a company on the stock market.

My business plan at that time was very simple – to grow the company by acquisition. I did this until 1974, when an investment bank wanted to gain control and I decided to sell. By that stage the novelty of owning my own business had started to pall and I felt I wasn't being challenged creatively. I sold out just three months before the property market crashed and interest rates shot up. It was more by luck than design, but it made me look like I knew what I was doing. At the age of 30, I had £1.6million in the bank and a pretty good reputation as a businessman. I thought I was unassailable.

Barred from the fashion business by the terms of the company sale, I started to go into other areas, starting a cocktail bar called Rumours in Covent Garden and dabbling in finance. Then I was asked to go back to run the company I had sold. 'Fine,' I told them. 'Just as long as you remove the original non-compete clause.' I was back in clothing, where I felt happiest. Over the next few years, I made a name for myself by buying companies and turning them around. Then, in the mid-1980s, someone asked me if I'd be interested in taking on the men's trouser business Honorbilt, a division of Austin Reed. Why not? I thought.

So in 1986 I bought it and in August 1987 we went public. Two months later, in October, there was the biggest market crash of all time. My shares dropped to 25 per cent of their original value. I had a lot of personal money invested in the company and it was a difficult time, but gradually the shares started to recover. However, we needed to take on a partner to underwrite the business, so we agreed to take on another company. Within a month we discovered that company had major difficulties and eventually, in 1990, we had to go into receivership.

It was horrible. After all those years of positive press, suddenly the papers were full of uncomplimentary things and it wasn't a pleasant experience. You start to think, Can I recover from this? For a while my home was in jeopardy, although luckily I managed to hold on to it. But you can't afford to think like that for long. Slowly I began the arduous task of clawing my career back. For a while in the mid-1990s I concentrated on bars and restaurants. Then I was headhunted by a Swiss company and ended up going to Germany for two and a half years to help an ailing company there. After that I was involved in buying the menswear division of the William Baird clothing group. When I took it over, it was losing money, but by the time I sold my shares four years later, it was profitable.

At the beginning of the present decade, I was starting to think about retirement. I'd had a colourful life, I'd made a lot of money – true, I'd lost it once, but I'd built it back up again. My children were both doing well – my son was running the restaurants and bars side of the business. Why not take it easy? But then came an offer I just couldn't refuse – Jaeger. The company was in trouble when I took over in 2003, but it was a brand that stood for quality, which is what I've always been about. In 2004, Belinda Earl joined me and in the past few years I'm really proud to say we have turned Jaeger around; now it's in an enviably strong position.

I'm also delighted to be chairman of the British Fashion Council. I'm still passionate about fashion and about nurturing new talent, which is why I've also sponsored scholarships at the London College of Fashion.

I know I could retire tomorrow, but I still have a drive to keep on working. My father was such a hard worker, and I think he instilled that same drive in me. I can see the same thing in both my children. Plus I surround myself with other people who have drive at work. And there's no such thing as too much financial security. I've made some losses in my life and I'm all too aware that when you've got financial security, you want to try to hang on to it if you can.

Starting a business from scratch is much harder now than it used to be, but if I had to give advice to anyone just starting out, I'd say you have to be realistic about your strengths. Flair is something you've either got or you haven't. You can't grow flair. Aside from that, I'd say just get on with it. Don't leave things until tomorrow. I'm a strong believer in getting everything possible done today instead of putting it off, because in business only one thing is certain – you never know what's coming next, as the world is now witnessing.

CHAPTER 12

DOMINIC MCVEY
I CAN HAVE THAT

Dominic McVey made the headlines at 15 when, working from his bedroom, he made a fortune developing and importing scooters. Now 23 and the head of Cosmagenics, a thriving cosmetics distribution company, he has learned a few important lessons from that early giddy success.

One thing I've discovered is that nature, not nurture, has a lot to do with how people turn out. I have very strong political beliefs and I've had very successful businesses. A lot of people look at my background and can't understand it. They say, 'Where do you come from? Where do your business and political ideas come from? Your dad's a musician and your mum used to be a model – how does that follow?'

The truth is I think I get a lot from my grandfather. My mum's dad was quite powerful in the electrician's union. After the war they sacked all the women who'd been doing those jobs while the men were away fighting and my granddad thought that wasn't fair. He started the biggest walk-out of electricians in recent times and got kicked out of the union for his trouble. And after it was all over, he couldn't get a job.

I'm very much the same as him. I get very angry at

segregation, sexism, racism, hierarchies or any kind of injustice. I get very passionate about causes. Maybe that's why business has always come easy to me – because I've got that perspective on business and money. They're not what I think about at night. They're not where my passion lies. They're a means to an end. My mum and dad are very good people but they never had that kind of passion about causes that I have.

I grew up in a very comfortable but very hard-working environment in Leytonstone, in east London. My dad's family is from Glasgow originally but he grew up in Walthamstow on a council estate. My mum grew up in a flat with her four brothers and sisters. So when they had me, they wanted to give me everything they didn't have, but not in a spoilt way, because they didn't have a lot of money.

I was always on the move when I was a kid. I didn't have ADHD or anything – I just had loads of energy. I walked early – well, I didn't walk, I ran. At nine months old I ran to the table and pulled the kettle off it. Boiling water went all over me, scalding my chest – I've still got the scars. All because I was running around the house at less than a year old. Sometimes people comment now on how laid back I am. Yet I don't stop eating and I never put on any weight. People say, 'It must be nervous energy,' but I'm not nervous. I don't know what it is, that inner drive, but it's always been there.

As soon as I was out of nappies, just before I was two, my parents sent me to a Montessori nursery because my mum just couldn't handle me. I was constantly demanding to know why. Why this? Why that? Why? Why? Why? I must have been completely exhausting. When I was four, they wanted to send me to primary school, but the local school wouldn't take me until I was older. My parents couldn't really afford to send me to private school, but they knew I couldn't stay at home, so my mum went back to work and my dad got a second job so they could pay the fees.

My dad was musical director at the Royal Shakespeare Company and its principal percussionist. If you have a job you love and you get paid for it, you're really lucky – that's something I learned from watching my dad. Usually you earn money from doing something you don't like. He had a great job. For a few months of the year he'd be touring the world. It was very prestigious and he was treated very well, and he won lots of awards. As a young man he'd won the musician of the year and a scholarship to Royal Academy of Music. He was a hugely talented musician, and still is. He retired about five years ago but he's teaching in schools now. He loves the energy the kids have. Anyway, to send me to private school, he started teaching during the day as well as performing in the evenings, and my mum started working in the Royal Shakespeare Company shop.

Private school was a big eye-opener. I'd be driven there in our Citroen 2CV and all the other kids were turning up in their Range Rovers. So from a very early age I noticed that people were looking at me because of what I had, or rather because of what I didn't have. I thought, Stuff you –

I can have that. At four years old I was already thinking, Just because you've got it doesn't mean I can't have it. It formed kind of an 'up you' mentality that has never really left me.

At school we were looked on as a crazy bohemian family, which I suppose we were. We were pretty unconventional, at any rate. I've got a half-sister who's 13 years older than me. Her biological dad wasn't around when she was growing up, so it was my dad who brought her up and walked her down the aisle. My mum had it very tough. My sister's dad had walked out on her. For two years all my mum could afford to live in was a camper van and worked for the Abbey National while she was living in it. They were always asking, 'What's your address?' and she didn't have one. But she worked bloody hard and within two years, she had a house. Mum is very determined and a grafter, and I get a lot from her in that respect.

Mum has had a really interesting life. She'd been a successful model at one stage, but she also used to work the market stalls before she moved to London to work for the Abbey. Years later we'd be watching telly and she would say, 'Oh, I know him.' I'd say 'Mum, that's Richard Branson! How on earth do you know him?' It turned out that he'd had the stall next to hers, selling TVs. Mum has always gone off and done her own thing, seeing the world, taking an interest in what's around her. She's 63 now and she still begs to come out to parties. Every time I see her, she says, 'Come on, let's go out. We're not staying in.'

Mum could also really raise the bar. She'd stand there

next to her 2CV outside the school gates, and somehow manage to be more snooty than the next person in their Bentley. Mind you, it wasn't a show. She had been on some of the biggest catwalks in the world, and when my dad travelled he went to all the different embassies or met royal families. They weren't intimidated by rich parents at a school. Instead they looked at these people and said, 'You may have more money, but you're not achieving the things in life that we're achieving in life by creativity.'

What was great about my education was that I went to school with very rich kids but I went home to a very normal lifestyle. That has helped me be able to fit in almost anywhere. In business now, you could take me somewhere that's not the nicest place in the world, and I would understand the culture, the way they're dealing with each other, and the way they're thinking.

I also grew up around adults, which is why I think I never had any fear of going into business so young. I was used to dealing with adults in an adult world. My parents always treated me as a person, not as a kid, so I grew up quite quickly. I never had a babysitter. Instead I used to go out with my parents. I'd go to work with my dad and he'd be playing a concert to hundreds of people and I'd have to not make a sound. Then we'd go out to dinner and I couldn't behave like a brat, because it was all adults. If I wanted to sit in the restaurant with the actors and actresses, people like Judi Dench, I had to behave. They all used to stay at our house. I didn't care who they were at that age, but I knew that if they were cool people who I wanted to hang out with, I couldn't run around throwing tantrums. Even my sister – who was the youngest person in my life – was well over a decade older than me, so I was always acting older than I actually was because I wanted to fit in with everyone around me.

Despite the sacrifices my parents made to send me to school, it didn't really agree with me. I got bored really quickly. I was the clown of the class and just wanted to make people laugh. I also had this heightened sense of injustice and I used to stand up for people. I hated it when anyone else got picked on and I certainly didn't go in for any type of bullying myself. I was just a pain in the arse. The teachers couldn't cope with me.

Then, when I was 12, they put us all into sets and they put me in all the bottom sets. That really pissed me off. You need to challenge the kids who aren't as smart and put them with the smarter kids so they end up coming up to their level. You put a bunch of not very bright kids all in one room and they're just going to start trouble. No one's ever going to improve because there's no one to bring them up.

But I didn't want to be in the top set either, because only the most geeky kids were in there – no friends, no social skills, never go out, locked in a room by their parents, talk to each other in funny voices all class long, talk to their rubbers on the end of their pencils... I was against the whole idea of separating people like that. I thought the whole system was disgusting. I just couldn't see the point. I remember the day I went back to get my GCSE results – all these kids were being punched and yelled at by their parents because they didn't get nine A*s. It's no way to educate children.

I was very good at mental stuff at school, thinking things through in my head. I'd always be shouting out answers but I couldn't do the written stuff, so there just didn't seem to be any point to me being there. Most of the time I was sent out of the classroom because I couldn't hide how bored I was. Why does a something get hot when you rub it? Well, why do you rub your hands together to get warm? Because of friction. Am I really going to spend two years learning that? I ended up virtually leaving school at 15, and only went back to do my GCSE exams. I went to two science classes in my whole two-year GCSE course, and I still got a C. It's not difficult.

To be honest, I don't really see the point of school after the age of 14. Fourteen is when your education stops. From 14 to 16, they're just keeping you in school for the sake of it. We should be talking to kids about mortgages, not making them learn the periodic table. I learned all about mortgages when I got my first one at 18.

Instead of focusing on lessons and learning, I turned my attention to business, which was far more enjoyable. I'd started my first business at eight – buying stuff in Japan and selling it to mates here quite cheaply. It was stuff you couldn't really get here like MP3 players and G Shock watches. My dad would get free tickets to Japan if he was working there and I'd go to see him. I'd come back with all this cool stuff and my mates would go, 'I want one of them,' and their dads would say, 'I want one.' So the next time I'd come back and sell it to them and charge their dads an extra £20.

It was fun. It *is* fun. When business goes well there's a real sense of achievement. When I went to Japan the first time, I was on my own and I got fed up because I was sat at the back of the plane, looking over everyone's head to see this one television screen. Bored, I got out of my seat and wandered around, and I was amazed to see there were guys at the front with their own screens. When I met up with my dad at the airport I told him about these people and complained that it wasn't fair and said I wanted my own screen. He said, 'Oh, they're businessmen.' So I said, 'I want to be a businessman then.' And he said, 'Maybe when you're 30 and you've been to school and university, you'll be able to travel business class.'

Now, me as a person, I don't wait. I've never waited. If I want something, I'll do it. Not in a cocky way, but I just don't want to wait. Even as an adult, I don't think about the future or the past. I think about today. If someone says, 'Oh, this is going to happen in two weeks,' I won't think about it. I'll think about it when it happens.

I didn't want to wait 22 years to travel business class so I said to my dad, 'I want to travel business class NOW. What do I have to do?' He thought for a bit and then said, 'I'll get you a copy of the *Financial Times*.' He took me around the finance area of Tokyo and I started asking lots of questions. 'What about this shares stuff? How does that work?' He said, 'Well, I don't really know, but if I was going to buy any shares, I'd buy them in something I like. Because if I like it, other people are going to like it and then I think they might go up.'

There was a business card in that *FT* and I thought, Wait a minute – I should get a business card. So I kept that card, which was for a share-dealer. When I got back to the UK, I came into a bit of money, about £2,000. My dad had put away some money for me in a PEP, which had matured. I decided to buy a computer, which cost most of that, and I managed to get on line. Thirteen years ago there weren't that many people online but I was one of them.

I remembered that business card I'd kept, so I went to the share-dealing website and signed up with my dad's credit card, which I'd taken out of his wallet without him knowing. I bought shares in Psion because my dad had this handheld device called a Palm Pilot that I loved playing on, and I remembered him saying he'd buy shares in something he liked. Sure enough the share value went up and one day my dad got a call: 'Mr McVey, your shares have gone up. Would you like us to release a cheque? First we need to take you through security. We'd like to confirm your income is a million pounds a year and you drive a Ferrari.' He said, 'I think you'd better talk to my son.'

I got into trouble, but I made a few quid – about three or

four hundred pounds. It gave me a bit of a buzz, but my dad took his credit card away.

At the end of prep school, when I was 11, I organised a party and charged everyone a pound. I did quite well out of that, so I did it every year. I made a grand sometimes. With the proceeds from that I set up this website – an e-commerce site – but I needed products to buy. I needed stock. I looked around and I found a company that was manufacturing petrol scooters and was instantly hooked.

I was about 13 then and I liked the scooters because they looked cool, rather than from any business angle. I contacted the company and said, 'I've got a website and I want to sell your scooters on them.' They said, 'Well, if you buy five, we'll give you one for free.' It took me months to save up for these scooters, doing club nights and setting up websites for people. They were about £400 each and I had to wait until I had enough to buy them outright. When I eventually got the scooters in, I sold them all within a day. They were quite big clunky things, but no one else had them. Once I'd sold the original four, other people saw them and wanted them. I was selling them for £650, so that was a mark up of £250. It all mushroomed from there.

After selling the scooters for a while I wanted something cheaper and started throwing ideas around with a manufacturing company. They would come up with ideas and I'd say, 'I don't like this, I don't like that,' until eventually we came up with the idea of the fold–up microlite scooters. I didn't produce them, I just helped to develop and sell them. Those did phenomenally well. After eight months I was making big money. I think we eventually sold about 11 million scooters worldwide, both petrol and push.

My parents didn't really know how much money I was making – not until we travelled somewhere and I went business class! But it wasn't long before the press got wind of this story of this schoolboy making millions from his bedroom. I quickly got an understanding of what the press is and the value of promotion. I didn't mind – it was all good for the business.

But I didn't make as much out of the scooters as I should have done, because I didn't understand VAT and tax. I made probably about £7million, but if I'd known more about business it could easily have been about £30million or £40million. My mum took most of it and tied it up for me. It's still tied up and I try not to think about it. That strategy has worked well for me because I've gone on to set up other businesses, but if I'd been able to get hold of that money at that age I think I'd just have become a bum. It would have been like winning the Lottery. We'd probably have a nice house now with a pool and flash cars, but the money would have gone. And you know, we still have a nice house and cars, but I've built it all up again from scratch without having to dip into that money.

My dad was actually very scared of that money. He was worried I was going to get kidnapped. I eventually bought a couple of houses with it. I've now got a big property portfolio – about £4million worth. At that time I was still nominally at school, although by this stage I was only really going into school for music class. When I started my business the teachers would try to wind me up about it. They'd say, 'Made much money today?' I'd say, 'Only around ten grand. Not a bad day's work.'

When I was 16 I moved out of the family home to a flat in Mayfair and it all went a bit wrong. I was getting paid a lot of money by the government and various big companies to consult on setting up businesses. I was earning over £1,000 a day but I was only 16 – I didn't turn up, I messed around. I got the job done, but I wasn't professional about it. I thought I could do anything. I started buying or investing in lots of things I didn't know anything about, like festivals and restaurants. I was spending silly money and it was a very fast, very expensive learning curve. I lost a lot of money, which taught me I'm not an expert in everything and to employ experts for the things I don't really understand. You should always be the first to hold your hand up and say, 'I can't do it.' Don't let someone else come to you and say, 'You can't do it.'

While I was living on my own in Mayfair, I went really wild for about a year. There were lots of silly parties, very rock and roll. I wasn't a very nice person. My mum would get all the credit-card and bank statements and come round and say, 'Where have you been spending this money? When did you go to America?' They were really worried about my lifestyle and they were right to be. I ended up in hospital. I was just worn out – I was too young to be dealing with all this stuff. I started suffering from anxiety, which makes you a recluse. In the end my mum took me home. I recuperated for a bit and then set out to take over the world again, which I seem to be doing pretty well now.

After you've burned out, which is essentially what I did, you can't afford to spend too long doing nothing. You've got to get back into the world again – get involved in something, it doesn't matter what. There's nothing worse than sitting at home watching TV all day. I used to go out and walk around, not doing anything in particular but just getting ideas for things. That's what I'm good at – looking at what's around me until an idea comes to me. I think I see things that other people don't see, and quite often I'm sure people think I'm mad, but that's OK – I'm in good company. When the guy who invented the wheel came down the street, everyone would have said, 'What an idiot, it'll never work.' When the guy invented a computer the size of a room, everyone said, 'What an idiot, it'll never work.' The guy that invented cats' eyes – he was probably called an idiot too but he made millions from his patent. If you're an inventor, you have to start off with the basic, most obvious idea, regardless of whether people think you're stupid.

After moving back home, I didn't sit in a darkened room willing myself to come up with an idea. I started going out discovering stuff – looking at ideas, looking at companies, seeing people. I needed the outside stimulus. Show me something basic and my mind will come up with something other people won't come up with. I don't think it, I just say it − it just comes out. Once an idea is out, it's just a question of connecting all the dots − it's there, it just appears. It's obvious. It's staring you in the face.

Those people who go on *Dragons Den* convinced they've got the next big invention are so often deluded because they're trying too hard. If their idea doesn't work it's because they've gone looking for it. They've convinced themselves it's good. It's easy to convince yourself. They've found this stick that turns red if you squeeze it. The whole day long they're going, 'It's amazing, it's amazing.' But just because you've thought of something doesn't mean it's amazing. The number of people who will convince themselves that something is a genius idea is beyond belief.

At the moment you have a whole country thinking, All these entrepreneurs, they've done it so easily − I know, I'm going to be an entrepreneur. Within two hours they've got the greatest idea in the world, and that's their idea and they're sticking with it. It just doesn't work like that. You can't force an idea to come. You've got highly trained inventors and they won't get a product made until they're 50. You see it in the movies: they'll be working on this bloody project and then one day at 2am it hits them in the face. That's what it's like.

How come I can do it? I don't know. There's no clear-cut answer. You've either got it or you haven't. Ask me to paint a watercolour portrait and I can't. My mind just doesn't work like that. But some people can do it. A lot of people have got something, some talent, but they do nothing with it. It's wasted. I think that's tragic. Life's short. You've just got to get on with it. Just do it.

I drive my car as fast as I can whenever I can. I know it's illegal and dangerous, but I like it so I just do it. You can't think about negatives. If you spend all day thinking, Oh God – I can't do that, you'll get nothing done. When I turn up to an airport, most of the time I turn up late. If I get on, I get on; if I don't, I don't. Most of the time I get on. If I don't, there's always another plane. Anything's possible. Just get on with it.

When I was 16 I started getting involved in cosmetics. I'd started consulting for a condom company in the Middle East, then I started working in pharmaceuticals. My girlfriend at the time was working for a cosmetics firm and complaining about it endlessly, telling me all the problems. I said, 'Well, I know how to fix it.' She said, 'But you work in pharmaceuticals.' So I said, 'Making pharmaceuticals is a lot harder than making a bloody lipstick.' And she said: 'Well, have a go then'. She gave me something to copy, and I copied it and I made it a lot better. That was for a company called Pout and I got a quarter-million pound contract out of it. I did a deal with a manufacturing company to make the products I came up with. I had that contract for about three years, up until about 18 months ago.

Towards the end of that period we set up a distribution company called Cosmagenics, which has gone very well.

Distribution suits me down to the ground. I understand distribution. I understand marketing. I understand retail. I understand how people want to be sold something, how they want to buy something, how they want it presented to them. The trouble with manufacturing is you have to wait 18 months to get your product. I don't want to have to wait 18 months. I'll wait 30 days, that's it.

These days I spend my time travelling the world, looking around for more products, but business is no longer the driving force in my life. I want to go into politics. I'd like to be an independent politician. I think a lot of people in this country are really fed up. I think I'm going to wait three more years, maybe get a plc off the ground first, then become a politician. I want to make change. I get really emotional when I think about it, because I know I can make a change in people's lives. I know what my story can do. I've had the letters, I've had the thank you's. Dads who've been unemployed for the last five years have read my story and thought, Stuff this, and are now running businesses and able to take their kids on holiday for the first time.

When I go to bed at night these days, I don't think about products. I don't think about inventions, I don't think about business, I don't think about money, I don't write songs like a musician would. I write policies and speeches. I'm still only 23, and I've got a lot of years ahead of me. I want to make a difference.

CHAPTER 13

HILARY DEVEY
MY MISTAKES HAVE MADE
ME WHO I AM

*One of very few female tycoons in the transport
industry, Hilary Devey, 51, has made her fortune from
providing a centralised pallet distribution network – but
at a painfully high personal cost.*

It's funny how some scenes stay with you for life. One of my earliest memories is of being in our house in Bolton and hearing a big commotion at the door. All of a sudden these men burst inside and started grabbing hold of furniture, ornaments, anything they could find, and hauling it all into a big lorry outside. I was only about six and of course I didn't understand what was happening. I could only watch, terrified, as they took away every single bit of furniture, including our beds, leaving just two orange crates for me and my little brother to sit on. I remember huddling at the top of the stairs with my brother and seeing my mother break down sobbing.

Much later, I found out that my dad, who'd owned a large central heating company, had gone bankrupt when his main client had gone into liquidation, and that the men who'd taken all our things away were bailiffs. Though I didn't know anything about that at the time, which would have been the early 1960s, a scene like that has a huge effect subconsciously. From then on, buried deep down inside me was always the thought, That's never ever going to happen to me.

After that episode we had to go to live with relatives, which must have been very hard for my parents. But they were very hard-working people. My father soon set up the central heating business again and also went into running leasehold pubs and hotels. He'd work on his own business during the day and in the evenings he'd stand behind a bar or a reception desk. He can't have got more than three or four hours sleep a night. My mother also put in long days working in the pubs and hotels.

My brother and I realised from a very young age that whatever you have in life, you have to work for it, and we spent all our spare time helping out. By the age of 11 I knew how to run a bar, and to take a reservations letter, type it up and post it out. By 12, I'd diversified into other avenues and was working 12-hour days at the weekends, running market stalls and ice cream vans. I knew that if I wanted something, I had to go out and earn it.

By today's standards, you'd probably think it was a hard upbringing, but we didn't resent it at all. We were a close, loving family and I never remember feeling unhappy. I suppose there were the usual tantrums, but nothing out of the ordinary. The only time I remember feeling resentful was when my father would favour my brother over me. He was old-fashioned in that way and he'd say, 'Your brother can go to university but you can't. It's a waste as you're just a girl,' or 'I'm not going to pay for driving lessons for you. When you get married your husband can pay for them.'

I left home at 16 and first got a job at a hotel in Llandudno, then spent 18 months in the WRAFs, which I loved. But when my father was diagnosed with stomach cancer, it tore me apart to be so far away from him, so I left and moved back home, where I quickly got married to my childhood sweetheart.

I was very close to my dad and his death affected me very badly. Even though I'd rebelled and pushed against the boundaries he set, he'd been such a huge influence over me. Before he got too sick to leave the house he had taken me out for a drink and told me not to stay with my husband. He thought I would be happier. Coming from a man who was very much of the 'You've made your bed, you lie in it' ilk, this was really revelatory. Once my dad died in June 1977, I made the decision to leave my husband and Bolton. I walked out of town with just the clothes I stood up in and a carrier bag full of my belongings. I would never live there again.

In those days I was tall, attractive and very sure of my ability to look after myself. I believed I would be all right, and I was. I went to London and got a job with a company that transported hanging garments for people and companies associated with the rag trade. That suited me down to the ground. I thought it was very glamorous because, even though it was a transport company and I was working in the accounts department, it was related to fashion.

At that point I didn't have any concrete ambitions, apart from to enjoy my life, but whatever I do in life I do it well and I was soon in a managerial position. I've always had tremendous amounts of self-confidence in my working life, whereas in my personal life I have next to none. I worked hard and played hard. I was there for nine years, one of the few women in the company. Somewhere along the way, I met my son's father and we lived together for seven years. I was so wedded to my job I remember I finished work on a Tuesday, had my son on a Thursday and was back at work six weeks later.

Work was my life – probably because of what I'd seen my parents go through as a child. After going as far as I was going to get in that first company, I went to work as sales director for a second employer and ended up as national sales manager for TNT, the massive transportation company. It was a huge job and I never stopped working. By that time I'd split up with my son's father and was a single mum, with all the responsibility for bringing up my son alone. I made a good living, but I worked for it.

I stayed at TNT for five years. I always knew I wouldn't stay there forever but in the end I had a falling out with the company and decided to set up on my own as a consultant. I was leaving a really good job with a good salary and security, but I felt sure I could do it. I wasn't scared of taking that move. I've never been scared of anything in my life really. I'm a strong believer in the old maxim 'As one door closes, another one opens.' I knew I'd be able to make a living.

For 18 months or so I really enjoyed the consultancy work. Sure, I missed the social interaction that comes with working in a busy office, and it was a shock to go from having several secretaries and controlling a workforce of hundreds, to working in isolation. But the flipside was I got to spend more time at home with my son.

Then came the moment that changed everything. I'd gone into a haulier's office in South Wales to advise them on something when I overheard one of the salesmen saying he could deliver a pallet of freight from Cardiff to Carlisle in 12 days. *Twelve days!* I could walk it quicker than that! I asked him why it would take so long and he explained how he now had to ring round all his customers and wait until they had enough orders to create a full load and then the driver would set off, taking a couple of days to get there. I thought, There *has* to be an easier way.

By the time I'd reached my car, my head was buzzing. All the way back home I was thinking it through. By the end of that weekend I'd come up with a basic idea that would become the business model for Pall-Ex – a network that would provide a next-day delivery service for palletised freight anywhere in the UK. I'd group the haulier members together geographically, each one covering a number of postcodes. Then we'd set up a distribution hub in the centre of the country, creating a hub-and-spoke model. Each member would send dedicated trucks to the hub every night, where the freight would be sorted by delivery area and assigned to the member responsible for the destination postcode. It would revolutionise distribution by speeding up the process and introducing unheard-of efficiencies, as well as saving costs.

Right from the start I just knew the idea would work. You have to have self-belief when you're starting any kind of business. You have to believe that failure just isn't an option. Then came the hard part of having to convince the individual haulage companies that it was going to work. I travelled thousands of miles around the country, visiting hauliers and talking to them about my vision. I never drove fewer than 2,000 miles in any one week. I'd be driving down the motorway and spot a truck with a haulier's phone number and address on the side and I'd think, I need a company in that postcode. So I'd grab the dictaphone I always kept on the passenger seat and repeat the number into it. When I got home I'd type up a letter and send it out.

I had one golden rule, however – I had to be home either to put my son to bed or get him up in the morning. Many a time I drove through the night just to make sure I kept to that.

In the meantime I had to raise funding to set up the hub where the pallets would be unloaded and reloaded. I'd done a business plan down to the last penny and knew I needed £112,000 to get up and running. When I went to show it to the bank manager, he all but patted me on the head, and more or less told me to run along back home and look after my child and forget about all this. I was so furious. By the time I'd got to my car, I'd thought, Stuff you – I'll do it on my own. I went home and put my house on the market and stuck a 'For Sale' notice in my car window.

Within months, I was living in a rented flat above a fish and chip shop in Southend. I had to put tin foil on the windows because it was so cold, and on a few occasions I even tin-foiled my son to keep him warm! My car was now an old banger, and I lived in constant fear of it breaking down. Several times I had to choose between feeding myself or feeding the dog. But I never once, for a single minute, thought, This isn't worth it. I had absolute faith that it was going to work.

By the time Pall-Ex launched on 29 November 1996, I had three main goals:

1 To give my son security, so we wouldn't need to keep moving every six months.
2 To give him a private education, as he'd been diagnosed as severely dyslexic.
3 To have a car that didn't break down.

Within a month of launching, I knew the company was going to be a big success. Nowadays there are several network companies doing what we do, but back then we were pioneers, and we're still one step ahead of the competition. In the 12 years since we launched, we've expanded our network abroad, taken on hundreds of members and moved out of the converted aircraft hangar where we started into a £12million state-of-the-art, purpose-built hub in Leicester. Within eight years of making that initial £112,000 investment, we were turning over more than £85million and it has just kept on growing.

Within a few months of starting out I'd achieved my three starting goals, so I kept replacing them with others – but always more to do with lifestyle than money. My father always said, 'Chase the money and it runs away,' and I believe in that absolutely. I live in a gorgeous country home in Staffordshire full of fabulous clothes and own properties in Spain and Marrakesh worth millions. If I sold up today I'd probably be worth £50million or £60million. But I'm as happy flying Ryanair as first class, and I'm as comfortable sipping a glass of wine in the local wine bar as drinking champagne in the Ritz.

Making a success of my business, particularly in such a male-dominated industry has brought me a tremendous sense of achievement, and has meant I'm in the fortunate position of being able to give money away. I've always been a philanthropist and over the year I've given away millions. Recently I was on the *Secret Millionaire* programme, living undercover in a run-down housing estate in Rochdale, and I handed over a big cheque to the community centre I volunteered at.

People say to me, 'Were you shocked at how people live?'

But the truth is, nothing really can shock me. My own son has been battling heroin addiction for years and let me tell you, when you've dragged your only child out of sordid drug dens in your pyjamas, you don't shock very easily.

In some respects being successful has turned out to be a bit of a poisoned chalice. You never really know if people are your friends because they like you, or they just like your money. If you asked me now whether all the sacrifices were worth it, I'd say, 'I don't really know.' Many times I've looked at my son and thought, Why have I done this? In a lot of ways I was happier before I got rich. When people ask what advice I have for those starting out, I say, 'Don't do it! And if you are going to do it, be prepared to make a lot of sacrifices.'

But the funny thing is that despite all that, I'd still do it all again – every single bit. I've made a lot of mistakes – but I needed to make those mistakes. I learned from them. My mistakes are as much responsible for making me who I am as my achievements. I've always lived my life at a phenomenal pace and I wouldn't know how to do it any other way. You can't go back, can you? You just keep on hurtling onwards.

CHAPTER 14

BRAD ROSSER
NOT JUST ANOTHER COG
IN THE WHEEL

*Brad Rosser, 45, has been right-hand man to
two of the greatest entrepreneurs – Alan Bond and
Richard Branson. Since then, he has carved himself his
own niche as king of the start-up businesses. To date he
has raised more than £1billion and nurtured and
sold businesses valued at up to several hundred
million pounds.*

In Perth, Western Australia, where I grew up, all anyone ever talked about was minerals and metals. That just didn't excite me. I was anxious to escape the humdrum Perth life as quickly as I could. I wanted to be different from my classmates, from my family. I didn't want to be just another cog in the wheel. I didn't want to be the guy turning up in the office every morning until it was time for the gold watch. I didn't know what I *did* want – all I knew was that it wasn't that.

I was always competitive at school, in a very focused way. I didn't want to be good at several sports – I just wanted to be excellent at one. I wanted to be the captain. I think the concept of the well-rounded individual is overrated. Don't be quite good at lots of things – be the top at one. Luckily I was a bright student, one of the top ones in the school. My dad, who was a civil servant, had been very academic and it was sort of expected that I'd go to university. That's exactly what I did, winning a Hackett scholarship – the University of Western Australia's highest honour – and then an MBA from Cornell University in the USA.

I didn't really have any clear ambitions at that stage, except that I wanted to go into business for myself and get rich. Not so that I could drive around in fast cars or yachts, but just so that I could have security. Once I had that goal of running my own business, everything else I did was a stepping-stone to get me there.

Soon after University I landed a job as executive assistant to Peter Beckwith, managing director of the Bond Corporation. At that stage the organisation – set up by the Australian maverick tycoon, Alan Bond – was a thriving, multi-billion pound operation and I learned a huge amount about making deals. Eventually I ended up as executive assistant to Alan Bond himself. I've never come across anyone as good as Alan at negotiating and picking the right industries to nurture, but there was a huge amount of ego involved and he over extended himself. Within a few years of me starting working with him, his empire had collapsed owing billions.

It was heartbreaking. One minute you're sitting next to one of the biggest entrepreneurs in the world, and the next minute it's all gone pear-shaped. But you have to pick yourself up and get on with the next step. Of course you allow yourself one night of having a few drinks, lamenting and feeling sorry for yourself, but the next morning it has to be gone. Never ever walk backwards. Just file that lesson away in the bank of what not to do.

I was lucky. Because I was so young and had been there a relatively short space of time, I didn't get tarred with the same brush as some others did and I had no trouble getting another job. I was taken on by McKinsey, the world's most prestigious management consultancy. I think they took me on because they love people with MBAs. Their theory is if you put enough smart people in a room, sooner or later they'll come up with something smart. I learned a lot about practical strategy and communication skills from them, but I knew I wasn't going to stay there long. Working for McKinsey was a long-term commitment – it would have taken ten years to make good money. People worked there to say that they worked there, not because of the money.

So when I heard Richard Branson was looking for someone to run new projects at Virgin, I went to see him. He didn't know me from Adam, but he took a chance. I worked for him at his Holland Park home in London, spearheading new ventures. It was a huge learning experience. Where Alan Bond had been peerless at picking industries, Richard Branson was fantastic at picking ideas.

By the time I left Virgin to start up businesses on my own, I'd had a pretty good training in how to be an entrepreneur. What was the most important thing I'd learned? That it's not rocket science. There's a lot of chance involved in becoming an entrepreneur, a lot of opportunity. But what marks the entrepreneurs out is that they take those opportunities, rather than thinking of all the reasons why they won't work.

It's the difference between theory and practice. You can

have all the theory in the world, but unless you put it into practice it doesn't mean anything. Entrepreneurs don't look for perfection before starting out. They take their business step by step and learn from real experience. Everything about being an entrepreneur is about forward momentum. You learn as you go. You just have to keep going forward. If you wait until something is perfect, you won't do it at all. Or else you'll do it and then discover you've got it wrong, because the only way to really test something out is to have customer feedback, and you can't do that without starting. Being an entrepreneur is as much about perspiration as inspiration. If you give it a fair crack of the whip and surround yourself with good people and keep going, you'll get there in the end.

People have this idea that entrepreneurs are inventors, but that's not usually the case. Yes, there are a few notable exceptions such as Bill Gates and James Dyson, but they're too rare to be role models. Most entrepreneurs take an existing industry or product and take it on to the next level. It makes sense – if someone comes up with a completely new idea that's radically different, you increase the risk of things going wrong. Whereas if someone comes up with an idea of how to improve something that already exists, it's much less risky.

What I specialise in now is start-ups. I'm an entrepreneur in as much as I go out and work on projects, but I see myself more as a business-builder. I get involved in a company during the first five years – my job is to grow it, get it mature, make it sustainable and then flog it. After five years, a company gets too corporate and I don't want to be involved. I don't want to be doing business from the golf course – that notion kills me. I'm out of there at that point.

Being in business for myself works for me. I think you've either got an employee mindset or an employer mindset. I've got good mates who go off and stay in five-star hotels paid for by their boss and they're really happy with that, but I'd rather own the hotels, or go into business with the hotel owner. I'd be thinking about my boss: I'm making this guy rich and he's paying me off with a first class trip to the Bahamas.

I always try to go into business with at least one partner, preferably someone who complements my skills. I take a chairman-type role – I'm the closer of deals and the ideas guy. I'm not the one who deals with the day-to-day stuff. I've always hated being told what to do. Even as a ten-year-old I couldn't stand it. And I can't abide office politics, so getting businesses off the ground works well for me. I still work as hard as I ever did, but I'm the guy who gets to say what I do. I drop my kids off at school every day, along with the mothers and the nannies, and it makes me laugh that all the other guys are stuck in an office somewhere.

So far I've raised over £1billion with start-up investments, so I think I've learned quite a bit about how to spot a successful idea. My advice to anyone starting out is, first of all, to be honest with yourself. Successful entrepreneurs never sugar-coat anything. Is your idea commercial? Is it in a growing market? Is it unique? Are there tangible benefits to justify it? Once you're convinced it's bulletproof, it's a question of just getting on with it. It makes me cry when people who've been developing and developing their business come to me and I say, 'Why have you got that state of the art IT and accounting system when you still have no customers?' You don't have to make it perfect, you just have to go out there and make sales.

You need to make a simple 'to do' list of things that will progress your business each day. Richard Branson used to run around with a little notebook with his 'to do' list on it. I really believe in setting goals – day to day, week to week and month to month. Bite-sized chunks. There's never a time when I don't have any goals. But you shouldn't make them airy-fairy, like 'be positive'. Make them practical – it's a 'to do' list rather than an inspirational list.

When things go wrong, as they will, don't personalise failure. You can't afford to think, Oh, it must be something about me. It's not about you. Just brush yourself down and get back to work.

Anyone can be an entrepreneur, as long as they're prepared to have a go. But you have to be prepared to put up with a certain amount of ambiguity. Going into business for yourself isn't clearly defined – it's not maths. There are lots of different answers, lots of balls in the air at one time. If you're someone who likes to come into work at a certain time and know what time you'll be leaving and be able to tick off the box that says three and three make six, being an entrepreneur isn't for you. But if you want to do something different, be something other than that cog in the wheel, have a go. What's stopping you?

CHAPTER 15

JENNY IRVINE
SUCCESS IS BEING HAPPY

In 2004, at the age of 27, Jenny Irvine launched her company, The Pure Package, with the simple concept of 'a diet to your door'. Five years on, the company is a huge success with thousands of clients, including many celebrities, having their tailor-made meals delivered to their door every day.

When they're children, most people already know what they want to do, and if they don't follow that dream they often end up leading very disappointed lives. Sometimes I ask people who want to work for me, 'What was your favourite game when you were little?' and if they say 'Lego' or 'Doctors and nurses', it's very telling. I think character and what you enjoy in life is formed when you're very little. I'm lucky in that I love what I do and it follows directly on from what I wanted to do as a child. I wanted to do something involving food, and I wanted to be my own boss. Now, as founder and CEO of The Pure Package, I've fulfilled those early dreams. How many people can say that?

My love of food comes from my upbringing. I was born in 1975 and grew up on a small farm in County Cork, in the southwest of Ireland. We were entirely self-sufficient but, as romantic as it sounds, the reality was very hard. My earliest memories are of churning butter, collecting water from the well and taking the cows in. It's funny because my two-and-a-half -year-old daughter is just learning to swim and I started thinking of what I could do at that age, and I thought, Well, I could make butter.

It was a deliberate choice that my parents had made. In the 1960s a lot of people chose to reject society and do their own thing, and that's what my parents did. My father used to lecture in philosophy in Trinity College, Dublin and my mother was a philosophy student at a different university. They met when he was given a guest lectureship and then they dropped out and decided to run their own farm. Everyone has a different set of criteria they live by. I think people often misinterpreted the way my parents lived, assuming they were trying to be environmentally friendly. It was nothing to do with that. It was just that they didn't see the need for putting curtains on the windows because they were happy to get up when the sun rose. It was an incredible way to be brought up.

There were four kids in our family and I was the second eldest. We were expected to help with everything around the farm. I never resented the way we lived and I always respected what my parents had done. Sometimes, though, it confused me when I was younger because I couldn't understand why they hadn't chosen a much easier path. I remember one day my mother said, 'I feel like some bacon' and my dad went out and killed a pig, knowing full well it would have been at least a week before you could get any bacon. My mother started to cry and said, 'Please, can't we just buy some bacon?'

I learned a lot from my parents. I learned how to cook and I learned how to look after animals. I learned those really valuable skills. They weren't interested in teaching us how to sail or how to ski. You grow self reliant and self-confident when you're brought up like that. You believe you can do anything and you can turn your hand to anything, because everything seems easy compared to what you've known.

My upbringing also made me very ambitious right from an early age, because as soon as I was old enough to visit other people's houses I knew this wasn't the life I wanted. Even though I shared my parents' ethical values to do with food and the way you treat animals, I still knew I wanted to have central heating. I remember staying with my cousins at their house in Dublin and being really surprised that they used to wear white clothes. As an adult I now wear a lot of white but as a child I couldn't, because nothing would ever stay white on the farm.

It's funny because an outsider might think I've rebelled against my parents in that I now provide a service that's the ultimate in convenience food. But I haven't lost the ethics that I learned from them. All the ingredients I use are from sustainable sources and my parents actually do approve of what I do now. I think we all realise that there are different ways of doing things, rather than just one right way.

I started my first business when I was eight. We had lots

of chickens and therefore lots of eggs. I used to sell my eggs to the local restaurants. By the time I was ten I'd moved onto selling chickens. By the age of 13 I'd branched out. I had a street trading licence and I used to sell T-shirts, or press flowers and put them in frames and sell them at different markets. It was fantastic preparation for setting up my own business as an adult. I had to keep accounts. I kept my own money and I learned a lot of valuable lessons. I lost my first big customer, a local restaurant, because some of the eggs had broken and she said she could use them anyway, so I didn't replace them. But she never ordered again, so I realised I should have replaced them, regardless of what she said. That's a valuable lesson in customer satisfaction – you have to always exceed expectations and keep your customers happy. I could have learned that when I was 30, but I learned it when I was eight.

My parents weren't ambitious for me. They were farmers and philosophers and cheese-makers. All they expected from us was to do our thing. They certainly weren't very interested in any particular marks that we got at school or how we did. I was not the best student in my class. Because of that I knew that if I went into other people's businesses, working for them, I wasn't necessarily going to come out on top. I was always an ideas person. Even as a child I always kept notebooks full of ideas. I still do. There are some you act on and some you don't. When I came up with the idea for The Pure Package, I thought, This is it! It's a great idea.

By the age of 12 I knew I would probably end up

working for other people but that I'd do better by myself. I think you should never underestimate these insights you have into yourself as a child. The Pure Package has lots of female customers who are big City lawyers. You look at these women and you know that if someone had asked them when they were a child, 'Do you want to do a job that means you're in an office 12 hours a day, working really hard?' they'd have said, 'Absolutely not.' For some reason people head down routes they never really intended to go down, mainly because of society's expectations of them. It's such a shame because you can do really well in a field that you're good at and you actually love.

I love food. It has always been my passion. I have a company that produces wonderful food and it happens to be nutritious, ethically sourced and helps people reach their health goals. It's something I'm extremely passionate about, and I think if people are doing something they love then, when those first awful hurdles come along, they're able to trample through them.

I enjoyed school, but it was always food and business that really inspired me. I learned a lot from my teachers who encouraged and celebrated individuality. In Ireland they have a kind of gap year between GCSEs and A levels where you have no exams, and during that year they encouraged us to set up little businesses. I ran the school tuck shop and the school bank.

At that time most people left Ireland at 18 because there were no jobs. Ireland was still a very poor country; when I left school unemployment was 19.5 per cent. I went to university in Reading to study food marketing economics, which is basically the study of how to recognise when the food market is ready for something.

As a student I used to run a soft drinks bar at a nightclub in Reading. It was a time when everyone was taking lots of drugs and not drinking alcohol, so the bars weren't doing very well. They had to increase revenue, so I had girls dressed like old-fashioned cigarette girls who used to walk around the nightclubs selling ice pops. We'd buy them for 8p each and sell them for 50p or £1. I made lots of money by doing innovative little things like that.

I also did some work experience at Sainsbury's and other big companies. I found these corporate environments interesting but my problem was I could always see ways to change things whereas people really just wanted me to get on with the job in hand. I also did some work for a London cheese shop called Neal's Yard Dairy as a Saturday job and when I left university I went to work for them full time.

I'm not a very confident person and I think I was too afraid of rejection to send out my CV and put myself through the process of applying for jobs at places where I wasn't known. I think that's why men do better in business, because from a very young age they're used to asking girls out and risking rejection, whereas women don't have that experience where someone is saying 'No. Leave me alone.' Men will go to their boss and say, 'Can I have a raise? Can I have a promotion?' Women haven't had that experience of exposing themselves to rejection so they don't try. I went to work at Neal's Yard Dairy principally because I didn't want to risk being knocked back. But it ended up being a very good experience for me and by the time I left I was the assistant buyer.

At the time I didn't realise just how much I was learning. One major lesson I took away from there was that it's easy to sell a product that tastes good and that you're proud of, because you can talk about it with pride. I also learned a bit about how to run a business. The staff were kept motivated by knowing what was going on in the organisation as a whole, being kept in the loop and being able to contribute ideas for how the organisation should run. That's the way I try to run things now.

After three and a half years, I was approached to work for a famous London company that ran a busy retail outlet and restaurant. I quickly became deputy manager, which meant that at the age of 23 I had 360 staff under me. It was a very steep learning curve because it was a very different organisation to Neal's Yard Dairies. But it wasn't a happy working experience. There were a lot of people in that organisation not working particularly well and there wasn't, in my view, sufficient accountability between the departments so it was next to impossible to do anything about it. It wasn't a tight ship.

From working there, I learned the importance of allowing managers to recruit their own teams and giving them some degree of authority over the people they're managing. In my organisation now, I'm really careful to keep my staff in the loop. I don't hide polices from the team. In too many organisations, people hide information from one another because they believe it gives them some sort of power. I just don't hold with that kind of ethos. I believe there can be a whole lot of winners. I don't do that whole dog-eat-dog thing. Life isn't about just one person being on the top. Lots of people can be on top. I believe life is all about being happy and you don't become happy by making someone else less happy. I'm only happy when everyone else around me is happy, and that's just not the sort of happiness I'm looking for.

After I'd been in that position for a year I was headhunted to work for another company as group development manager. It was my job to go into restaurants and turn them around by putting in new menus, new chefs, new management teams, or to give the current teams some support. You could see people who, despite being paid very little on paper, had incredible lifestyles. It became clear there was something very wrong in the organisation.

I tried to turn it around by getting the individual restaurants to do their accounts on a monthly basis. I showed them how to price up their menus. I did something that to them was totally bizarre, which was to find out the cost of the ingredients and then work out how much they should be charging for the dishes. I also moved managers between the different restaurants so they could share their experience and their expertise.

That taught me a lot about how to treat people. At The Pure Package, I make sure all the suppliers are paid on time so we have a good reputation and so we can negotiate to get the best quality of everything. We don't hold out until the last minute to pay people just because we think we're going to make a little bit of extra interest at the bank. A lot of companies have credit controllers who insist on withholding payment until the last minute. I think you're better off spending their salaries on paying people on time. It makes sense.

I worked for that second organisation for six months, getting increasingly stressed, and then had a mini revelation. I thought, this is ridiculous. I am going from bad to worse with my career. This is completely wrong for me. I could see my whole life unfolding in front of me if I stayed in that kind of environment, and I knew it wasn't the life I wanted. Not only that, I was in a relationship I also knew deep down was wrong. All I wanted was to be happy. I felt my integrity was being compromised on all sides. This was just not where I wanted to be.

I had a little bit of money in the bank and almost overnight I sold my London apartment, broke up with my fiancé and bought a ticket to Asia. Why Asia? I knew it was cheap to travel there and had met people who'd travelled there alone. After everything was paid off I had £3,500 and, though I probably ought to have been nervous, I was only excited.

The first thing I did when I went away was to write a list

of what I wanted from life. Top of my list was a family. I was 24, and I thought, I'm done with parties. I want to have a family. I want to have children and a husband. The trouble was, I didn't see myself as being good wife material. I couldn't see why anyone would choose me (that old self-confidence thing again). So I decided I'd work on making myself a more rounded person. In the six months I was away I took courses in massage and scuba diving and oriental cookery. I studied yoga, sailing and diving. I had incredible fun.

The trip abroad changed me in fundamental ways. It made me reassess my life and think about what I actually wanted, and how little things like money actually matter because it's all relative depending on where you are in the world. I also realised that I wasn't going to be happy unless what I did had integrity. If you don't have integrity, you're just going to fall at every single obstacle. If an organisation is in some way dishonest, there's no way they can jump any hurdles when they come along. Instead they just think, Well we should have fallen a long time ago, and give up.

When I returned from Asia I ended up keeping house for a friend who was a very high-powered businessman, but very disorganised at home. I did a bit of part-time temping work, and then I met my husband. He works in the City but he values his privacy, so I don't really talk about him.

When my husband moved to New York with his company I went with him and because I wasn't legally allowed to work in the US, I became a lady of leisure. I used to spend my days coming up with lots and lots of new business ideas, and eventually I came up with the idea for The Pure Package – a diet delivered to your door. The basic concept was to supply meals that are fresh and delicious but tailored to help clients reach their health goals. We'd make breakfast, lunch and dinner – and deliver it to the client's door each and every morning. It was to be ultimate convenience but with a conscience. I wouldn't use chickens from factory farms or eggs from factory farms or anything genetically modified and we'd use a lot of organic ingredients.

There were similar companies in New York doing similar things but I tried them and knew they wouldn't work in London because the standard of food wasn't good enough. I would have to do a lot better than that.

We were in the US for a year and a half, and by the time we came back I'd already done all the horrible nitty-gritty stuff for my fledgling company, like working out a computer system. The first thing I did when we got home was to call the local Environmental Health & Safety officer and say, 'Come round and tell me what you think of my kitchen. Can I start from here?'

I didn't have the confidence to go to a bank manager and ask for a loan, so I had to start small. I think if I'd have had to ask for money from people like bank managers or venture capitalists – who'd ask me a whole list of negative questions and then most likely reject me anyway – I'd never have got started, so I didn't put myself in that position. I knew that as a woman of child-bearing age, I'd be asked, 'Well, what are you going to do when you have kids?' I had no idea. I was a pioneer. At that time no one else was doing specially prepared food delivered to your door. So I had to do everything on a small scale, based on what we already had – a kitchen and a computer. I also had some savings, about £10,000, which I used to get advice on menus from a nutritional therapist.

Launching the company in 2004 wasn't scary because it happened in a very organic way. I had already tested out all the food. I used to have friends come round and try things and ask for their opinions. Next, I sought the opinions of the most opinionated people in the world – journalists. I invited them to try the food and made it clear it wasn't for a piece. I just wanted them to fill in the forms about what they thought of the cutlery, the presentation, the smell. A couple of them did actually write pieces, and from those pieces I got my first clients.

I knew right away the business had a huge chance of success because the phone rang off the hook. I made a conscious decision that instead of trying to take all the callers on and run the risk of messing up, I'd do things properly – get them to fill out an application form and put them on a waiting list. Even today that's what we do if we get a glut of customers. One of my first clients was a Michelin-starred chef. Then the second day after we launched properly I had Patsy Kensit on the phone. At that stage I already had a waiting list because I only had capacity in my fridge-freezer for ten clients. But she was really keen and I did take her on.

In the beginning it was just me devising menus with a nutritional therapist, then when we started having actual clients, I had a former colleague come and help me with the cooking. To put it in perspective, I was answering the phones, doing the deliveries – I used to drive round in my car in the middle of the night dropping off bags of food to people – and then during the day I'd do the cooking. I had so many ideas, I'd jump out of bed to write them down. I was going to bed with my husband and waiting for him to fall asleep, then running downstairs to do ideas and getting back in bed just before I knew he was about to wake up.

It very quickly became obvious I would need to raise more investment capital so we could expand and move the business out of the house. Again, I didn't want to go to the bank, so we raised the money from our customers. People were paying up front for ten days of food which was about £300, so I'd offer them a discount if they paid upfront for 30 days or 90 days and I used this money – closer to two or three thousand pounds a person – to get premises in New Covent Garden Market. The customers were all for paying up front. They'd already tasted the food, so they knew it was wonderful, and if you offer someone more of something that's wonderful, they'll think it's marvellous.

Our clients don't fit any particular mould. We have people like Ruby Wax who ring and say, 'I want to fit into a size eight dress for the BAFTA awards please' or others saying, 'I want to get a part in this movie.' But the thing is, unless there's something very wrong, it's actually quite easy to help someone achieve their health goal if you're making them breakfast, lunch, dinner and snack. It's not that big a deal. Imagine if you were weighing and measuring out each meal you had – you're going to achieve your goal.

That's why we don't have an issue with people saying they want to lose five or six stone. Not a problem. Obviously we can't check that they're not nipping round the corner for a bar of chocolate but we give them enough snacks that they shouldn't need anything else. We work around the clients' lifestyles to make sure it works for them. Obviously they have to have some degree of self-restraint, but they're not even having to go to a supermarket to buy food, so they're not coming in contact with temptation.

Some people might think our service is expensive, but it's not really when you work it out. If someone is a busy professional, they're easily spending £20 or £30 a day on their food. They go to Starbucks for breakfast, Pret a Manger for lunch and order a take-out for dinner. Also, so many people throw a lot of food out because they don't eat it by its sell-by date. With our service there's no waste.

Today we've got a couple of thousand clients and the list keeps growing. Our turnover in the first year was £192,000. This year we're looking at £1.5million. But more than the money, running my own company has brought me the happiness and balance I've been looking for. I now have three little girls so I spend a lot of time at home and only come into the office two days a week – though I still have my food delivered to my home every day!

One of the main reasons the company has been able to grow in the way it has is that I'm not a control freak. I'm the director of the business, not its lifeblood. It functions perfectly well without me. There was one incident that made me decide to take that step back. Three years ago, when I was six months pregnant with my eldest daughter, I was attacked and left with a broken leg and finger. I was going into my house in Notting Hill and as soon as I opened the door, this man pushed me inside, cracking my head against the wall and holding me. I think he was going to rob me, but my husband heard me kicking about and the guy fled. The ridiculous thing is that if he'd just have asked me for money, I'd have handed it over.

That attack changed me fundamentally. Now I don't see the point in taking any chances. For a long time I didn't go out at all and risk something bad happening again. I realised the world is actually a dangerous place and there are some horrible people out there, and I couldn't see the point of ever leaving my house. So I became a recluse.

I can now go to the supermarket and things like that but it's taken years. At one stage, a year and a half after the attack, my husband and I were buying a new DVD player in Tottenham Court Road. I went out into the street to walk to the next shop and all of a sudden it hit me that it wasn't safe and anything could happen to me. This was in broad daylight and of course it was perfectly safe, but I just became petrified. I sank back against the wall, completely terrified, and edged my way back to the shop where my husband was.

I still have problems with my leg and my finger, but the psychological scars are what really bother me. I will never trust human beings to the same degree again. However, being forced to stay inside my own house all that time did have some advantages. For a start I fell in love with my own products, because every day a bag was delivered to my door containing my breakfast, lunch, dinner, snacks, everything, so I wouldn't have to leave the house. I also had to let my team get on with their jobs. I've got a huge amount of respect for my team. I know they can do their jobs, so why not leave them to it?

I've never gone back to the company in the same way as before. I'm not as hands on now. Whenever there's an emergency I'm not the person who runs out in the middle of the night any more. When someone's off sick in the kitchen I don't necessarily step in and start peeling carrots. What happened to me helped me to get my work life balance right. Before I'd be thinking, My business needs me, every hour of every day. Nowadays I'm more interested in making sure the company is running in the right direction and looking at things more strategically, which has probably contributed to the success of the company.

I have masses of ideas for the future but I'm not going to act on them just yet. I've been told a million times: you should launch your muesli onto the market, you should launch your cereal bar onto the market. But there are so many products out there, why would I go those routes? Right now I'm concentrating on doing what we do as well as we possibly can, and when the time is right we'll expand into other areas. I'd love to be able to use what I've learned about food and diet to help more people, so at some point I'll probably be looking at doing a cookbook or a TV show.

At the moment, though, I'm very happy. I've got a lovely family, a business I love and a good work-life balance. My motivation was always purely to be happy. I could work 24 hours a day, 7 days a week if I wanted to. But that's not the lifestyle I've chosen because to me that's not success. Success is being happy, and happiness is something I only attain when I have a good balance in my life. I think life is a journey and happiness is relative, even within your own life. I know there's so much more to come.

CHAPTER 16

TONI MASCOLO
THE BUSINESS OF FAMILY

Toni Mascolo, 66, arrived in England at the age of 14, with nothing but a talent for hairdressing and a dream of building a business. Today TONI&GUY, the company he set up with his brother, is global and his fortune is put at more than £200million.

E ver since I was a young boy, I've had a passion for
   building. When I was growing up in Scafati, just south
of Naples, I used to collect things like old coins or little
pictures and carry them to a hiding place in the house
where no one else went. There I'd spend hours on end
building up my collections, getting so much satisfaction
from watching them grow. Years later, when I started my
own business with my brother, it was exactly the same
feeling. The enjoyment I got from expanding the company,
and seeing it build from the first salon to a global brand was
tremendous. More than the money or the fame, it was
about the process of building up a successful company step
by step.

   I got my hairdressing flair from my father. He was a
talented barber as his father had been before him. He had a
thriving salon in our home town and was a very popular
figure. One or two hundred years previously, barbers in Italy

hadn't just cut hair, they had been entertainers and physicians too – amputating limbs and pulling teeth – and my father had that flamboyant, larger than life persona. But my mother's family were merchants and lawyers – professional people – so they considered themselves a step above. That's why they put iron bars on the windows when she was younger to keep my father away from her.

In fact, I'm a mixture of both parents – a hairdresser but also a trader. It's a really good combination of the creative and the commercial. My father made a lot of money but he also spent a lot of money. He didn't have any notion of financial planning. His salon was always busy and he opened a couple of other salons outside of Scafati, but he had no bigger picture. That is so important in business – to be able to see where you're going.

We were a large family – I was the oldest of five brothers – so it was a noisy household. There was a lot of love in our family and a lot of warmth. I remember my father would come home and fling money down on the table and say, 'Come on, let's go out and celebrate!' My mother was a lady of her times. She was very stylish, always with her hair perfectly done and immaculate clothes. And she always made sure her family looked smart too. She was a very special person.

I loved school and learning. What really stands out in my memory is studying the diaries of Julius Caesar. He was a role model – he was a strategist and a planner and he was the master empire builder. Now that I've built a world company from nothing, I understand how important strategy is if you want to carry on expanding.

After school and at the weekends I'd often go to my father's salon to help him. I learned all the techniques there – shampooing, perms. I loved it all. I found it relaxing, not like hard work at all. I was a quiet sort of boy – not showy or demanding – but I was very interested in making sure things were fair. If I thought my parents had spent too much time with my brothers, I would say, 'It's my turn!' I had a burning sense of justice, and even back then I was very concerned with security. If my father asked me what I wanted, I'd always say, 'No, you save your money.' I've always been careful. Even today when we've got hundreds of salons and exciting new product ranges, security is still uppermost in my mind.

In Scafati, there wasn't much room for expansion. My father had his salons, but it was a small place and there wasn't anywhere else he could have progressed, so he began to feel frustrated. He had an old friend who'd moved to London and set up a salon with a coffee shop in Knightsbridge. This friend came back to Italy for a visit and said to my father, 'You must come to London. It's fantastic.' He described all the famous people who came into his place – Gina Lollobrigida, Sophia Loren, a famous countess and many other well-known celebrities. He told us he had so much money that he travelled to work by helicopter. That last one turned out to be an exaggeration, but it didn't matter. My father was won over.

So in the mid-1950s my father went to London for a while and worked in the salon of this friend. It was the place where the Italian stars of the time went to get their haircut. My father was staying in a flat in Kensington and living the high life, so of course he loved it. My mother went to visit him and it all seemed so glamorous, so she really liked it too. That was it. We were moving. I was only 14 so I didn't have a choice. Even though I was only two or three years off going to university, there was no one in Italy I could have stayed with so I could carry on at school. I had to come to England.

You can't imagine how it was to come to London in 1956 from a small town in Italy. After I'd arrived at Dover, my journey to London by train was like going to Disneyland, seeing all these beautiful little houses with neat little gardens, I could not believe what I was seeing. And of course London was a world-famous city. I was seeing buildings and sights I'd only ever seen before in films. It didn't seem real.

It was hard to make sense of the comparisons at first because there were good and bad things on both sides. When I came over here I saw the tremendous opportunity in the UK and the discipline and the strength here, compared to the chaos in Italy. But then in Italy you had the latest clothes, while England at that time was quite dowdy. And Italy had pizza, Peroni, cinemascope and there was no class distinction, unlike here.

I went to the Italian school in Clerkenwell. It's called the

Italian school but really there were children from everywhere. It was very difficult for me – I didn't speak a word of English. I'd been such a good student at school back home in Italy, and now there was almost no point in me being in the classroom because I couldn't understand what was being said. Because I couldn't speak English people assumed I wasn't intelligent, and yet there were children in my school who could hardly write well or do any of the things I'd known how to do since I was four. It was deeply frustrating.

I left school when I was 15. There wasn't any point in staying longer. If I'd stayed in Italy I might have gone to university and become a lawyer or something like that, but there's no point in regretting things that are past. Recently I was back in my home town and the boys I was at school with had gone on to great things – become judges and mayors. That was what you did there, but in England everything was different. The thing I realise now is those kind of social distinctions are not so important after all. You can have all the education in the world but you also have to have integrity.

Life was hard for us when we first moved to London. We lived in a basement flat in Islington with the seven of us cramped together. It was damp and we had to have the coal fire on all the time because it was so cold. It was a big change from our home in Italy, and it must have been very hard for my mother because she didn't go out to work and she spoke very little English, so she was in the flat a lot of the time. But she was an amazing woman. It upset me to see the efforts she had put in to make that flat as much of a home as she could. I made a promise that when I was older I would buy her a house. It is the big regret of my life that she died before I could do that.

When I first left school I worked with my father at a salon in Mayfair. It was run by a family friend who ran the men's side and leased the ladies' side to my father. London at that time was a very exciting place, especially for a young man from a small town in Italy. Working in the salon, I met all sorts of people – Malcolm Muggeridge, Alfred Marks, Christopher Lee. One time the famous hotelier, Charles Forte, put a pound note in my pocket and said, 'I hope this is the start of your career.' I was earning much less than that for a whole week, and was overwhelmed by that gesture.

Mayfair in those days was a very expensive area for exclusive clients and as an apprentice I needed more experience in the trade. I decided there would be more opportunity for me at a local salon to practise what I'd been learning, so I left to work for a company called Gerrards, doing cut-price perms and shampoo and sets. During my interview I was asked if I could cut hair, perm hair and tint hair. To my surprise, I was then hired immediately and made the manager of their Stockwell salon at the age of 16. I had a team of five working for me, another 16-year-old called Monica, a top stylist, an assistant and two Saturday girls. We were very, very busy doing lots of perms and sets from morning to evening and I gained lots of experience.

But always I wanted to keep moving forward. I wanted to improve myself so I went to work for a hairdresser called Lorenzo at 37 Victoria Street. He was in his mid-seventies when I started there, but we had a very good rapport. He taught me how to make permanent waves, use peroxide, make setting lotion, eau de cologne and hair lacquer. I also learned how to do PAYE, accounts and generally how to run a business.

It was very hard work. I started at eight in the morning and finished at nine in the evening. On Saturdays we were supposed to finish at one, but as I had clients coming in all the time I chose to work late. Of course, I had an incentive – the more I did, the more I earned – so I'd finish at five or six. My objective was to buy my mother that house and I was always working towards that.

As we were situated so close to Westminster, we had clients like Irene White MP, Barbara Castle MP and Mrs May, the wife of the secretary to the Prime Minister, Sir Alec Douglas-Home. Mr May had also been the secretary to prime ministers such as Sir Winston Churchill.

On one occasion Mrs May invited me for tea at her apartment at No 10 Downing St. On the way there, I asked the taxi driver to stop in Whitehall so I could make the rest of the way on foot because I was very nervous. When I arrived at No 10 I was terrified but eventually plucked up the courage to knock on the door. I remember so clearly being confronted by a huge policeman who said to me, 'What do you want!' I said, 'I have an appointment to see

Mrs May.' He then called her and we accompanied her to her apartment for tea and biscuits. As the Prime Minister was away at the time, Mr May showed me around the building from the staircases to the cabinet room, a truly amazing experience. Imagine me – an Italian boy – in the heart of the British Government!

Just to put it into perspective, at that time I was earning about £60 or £70 a week. An average civil servant's wage was about £12. For a 19-year old boy, I was doing really well. In fact, it was an absolutely amazing time for me. I was making money, I was productive, people were very proud of me. My boss was so happy with me that he offered me 50 per cent of the company. But there was a problem. My father had come to work there too, but the two men didn't get on very well because they were both very experienced and set in their own ways. Mr Lorenzo said, 'If your father retires early, I'll give you half the business.' I couldn't do that. Family comes first. Family is paramount. I've always believed that, so I left and started my own salon with my brother.

Years later, I went to see Mr Lorenzo and he said, 'I have to tell you something. I worked for nearly 50 years and in that time I managed to buy one flat. You worked for me for two years and I bought dozens of houses.' That has really stuck with me. That gave me such a sense of achievement.

Right from when I first started working, I began acquiring things. I was always thinking about long-term security and I knew property was a sound investment. At 17

I bought my first flat – 50/50 with my dad – and my first car, an Austin Cambridge. That was in 1959. I was very keen on having concrete things that represented security. The only thing I failed to achieve in my life was buying my mother that house. Even today I can't believe I didn't manage it. I really did try and I was very close to it, but sadly she died before I could realise that dream. She was only 45 and her death, as a result of a minor operation, was a huge blow to our family.

By this time we had moved from Islington to south London. She hadn't been well for a while but fortune tellers in Italy had warned her that if she had another operation she'd die, so she allowed herself to get very weak. She had a gallstone and the doctor came one morning and said, 'You have to have it removed now' – it was an emergency. I was there at the time and took her to the hospital. I was used to accompanying her as I could speak a little bit of English and I was the oldest. But that morning I could sense something horrible was going to happen. I could feel it. It was a very simple operation to remove the gallstone from her bladder, but because she was so weak, her heart would not support her and she died.

I was very badly affected by her death. She'd been such a central figure in my life. She'd been the person who really held our family together and we were all so lost without her. It became really clear to me around this time that we were going to have to do something, some business venture, to pull our family back together now that she'd gone. The only obvious choice was to start up our own salon so I left Mr Lorenzo, even though I was very happy there and I saw a great future.

My brother Gaetano had been working in a salon in Clapham owned by an older barber. It was in a terrible, shabby condition, all yellowing walls and peeling paper. 'Take it off my hands. I'll give you a 21-year lease for £20 a week,' the owner told me. I knew it wasn't worth £20 a week then – it probably wasn't even worth a tenth of that. But we wanted somewhere we didn't have to put up any money up front. And you know, 20 years later, we were still paying £20 a week, so it was worth it in the end.

Anyway, there was another reason for me deciding to take the place on. When I went to look around, I saw this girl there and thought, She's really lovely. I thought if we took over running the salon, I'd get to meet her. When we started there – me, my brothers and my father – all the staff who'd been working there left within days. I think they were scared by the idea of working for a bunch of Italian men. Only Pauline stayed. She was 15 at the time, and we've now been married for over 40 years. I'm as much in love with her now as I was on the first day I saw her.

I learned two things about Pauline very quickly – she will give anything to anyone and she will believe anything anyone tells her. When she was working for me a lady came in and Pauline told her she should have a perm. The lady said she didn't have enough money, but Pauline said, 'Oh, I've got time, I'll just do it anyway.' The next day a different woman came in, asking, 'Which is Pauline?' When she found her, she said, 'I'd like a perm, but I can't really afford it...' Luckily, I was in love with her by then or I'd have been tempted to let her go – she was costing me so much money!

We needed a name for the salon and like many people at the time, we wanted to call it after ourselves – but Giuseppe (my childhood name) & Gaetano didn't sound like the catchiest name. So, having been nicknamed Tony at one of the salons I worked in, I decided to adopt that, Italianising it slightly by changing the 'y' to an 'i'. Gaetano became Guy, so we were TONI&GUY.

We were busy almost from the start and because the Clapham salon was so tiny, people used to queue outside to have their hair cut – one in, one out. I think it was the atmosphere in the salon that attracted people. We were a family outfit, so we were all working for each other and with each other. That made it a really friendly place and it's the trademark of what TONI&GUY is today. I remember one time a client was waiting to have her hair cut and she said, 'Toni, I can see you're really busy. Shall I make us both a cup of tea?' This was real old-fashioned customer service in reverse, and the reason she offered was because she felt like she was a guest in our salon.

At that time, our brother Bruno wasn't hairdressing – he was in the fruit and vegetable business. My mother's side of the family had been merchants, and I think he had that blood flowing through him. He'd drive around trying to sell produce to the shops and restaurants. But he was a young man and he soon started comparing his life to ours. He said to himself, 'I have to get up at 5am, work all day and make very little money and there they are starting at 9am and enjoying themselves with all the pretty girls.' So he decided to join us as well, but he never lost that interest in trade and commerce.

We were young and full of ideas. Guy was very artistic – more than I was. He was a very strong salon hairdresser and a very good-looking boy. The ladies loved him, to the extent that my father used to say, 'All we need to do is put him in the window and we'll be busy all the time.' My younger brother Anthony was also extremely artistic and very daring. He had no fear about cutting hair. I was more serious and businesslike. Bruno was strong in public relations, and later on my brother Andrea was in accounts. So we were five boys with very different skills, complementing one another, and with my father's experience we made a perfect team. All of this combined is what made us so different from everyone else.

Very quickly we wanted to expand the business. At that time my role model was the celebrity hairdresser Raymond Teasy-Weasy, who had a chain of salons. I wanted to follow in his footsteps and have our own chain, and before long we found more premises in Streatham. My father, Bruno and Anthony went to work in Streatham, while Guy and I stayed in Clapham. There was a big Italian community in Streatham and with my father being his usual flamboyant self, it didn't take long for the salon to become extremely popular, particularly as it was unisex, which was unheard of in those days. Soon after that we opened the third salon in Tooting.

My father, my brothers and I divided up the workload for the salons between us. We worked really hard and the salons were busy all the time, so we all became very well known locally. Every Sunday we'd go to the cemetery where my mother was buried and as we drove through the streets of south London, practically everyone we passed was a client and they'd all recognise us and wave. It truly was an amazing feeling.

As the salons in Clapham and Streatham were family run, they worked really well. We were all working as a team and helping each other to be successful and make good profits. However when we opened our third salon in Tooting, we put it under management and that became a totally different situation. We didn't have the infrastructure or experience to have a chain of salons – it was too early for us. Although we were getting customers through the door and making good money, some weeks there just wasn't any money left after paying the staff and the rent. We had a good reputation as skilful stylists, but we weren't making the profits we'd hoped for. It was then that we decided to move to the West End.

At that time London was changing and becoming much more international. There were Japanese coming in and lots of wealthy Iranians. We felt we needed to find different, upmarket premises to suit the new times. I stayed behind in the Clapham branch to hold the fort while my brothers and father opened a new salon in Davies Street, Mayfair. It was near the Italian embassy, the American Embassy and Saatchi & Saatchi – right in the centre of London.

We did lots of publicity in *Girl About Town* and *Ms London* and soon we became known for our innovative styles. We changed the face of modern hairdressing by creating strong geometric cuts and very soft feminine looks, utilising lots of layers. This soon became very popular, especially the long, layered look, which was later adopted by the stars of *Charlie's Angels*. We also created a short, layered bob haircut, later made famous by Joanna Lumley. The hairstyles we created were very feminine and wearable and soon TONI&GUY haircuts became instantly recognisable.

The impact this had on our business was amazing and we became fully booked every day. Unlike in Clapham, where an appointment system was not necessary as people queued in the street, we now had a waiting list for our clients. Other hairdressers would also come in to our salons with photos of our hairstyles, telling us that everybody wanted these haircuts and that this had had the knock-on effect of making them busy as well, so they too were fully booked for weeks on end.

Moving to the West End was an important move for us. After we'd opened the first salon, the shop next door became available and we acquired that one as well. Don't forget that in those days, being Italian and having no connections meant that getting leases was almost impossible. We managed through sheer perseverance and will. Before long we had sold the salon in Tooting, then the one in Streatham. We wanted to move away from those links and create a fresh, new image, though we kept the salon in Clapham until the council bought it on compulsory purchase.

Then we decided to go back to our roots and go international, opening a salon in Rome. We had eight or nine years' worth of money saved up for this venture. It was an amazing salon, years ahead of its time, and Bruno went out there to take charge of it. But in some ways it became a victim of its own success. There were different ways of doing business in Italy and there was a bit of corruption there, and Bruno wasn't used to it. He called me one day and said, 'I don't feel as Italian as I thought I was.' He wanted to come back to England, which he did, leaving his business partner to run the salon. The partner wasn't happy. He felt betrayed and ended up having a kind of breakdown, so his wife became the administrator. The whole situation was a mess and it took ten years of legal action to get the name back from the salon in Rome.

At the time it was a tremendous blow – a disaster like you could never imagine. It seemed like the end of the world. We'd worked for 15 years and suddenly it was all gone. But sometimes the biggest disasters can actually turn out to be the greatest opportunities, because after all that was over, Bruno ended up going to the US and becoming a big success. If he'd stayed in Italy he'd probably have grown to a certain level and stopped, but in America there was nothing to stop him – no ceiling, no limits.

Sometimes the same thing happens when there's a recession. You think it's a total disaster but it turns out to be a real opportunity for strengthening your thinking and sorting out the basics. But you never know that at the time – only ten or 15 years later. That has happened to me many times in my life.

Even though we were more or less starting again, I never felt like giving up. I still had the bigger picture in my head. We opened another salon in Sloane Square and Bruno came and worked there. That's where we really cemented the brand and reputation of TONI&GUY. We put our staff through such a rigorous training procedure, it meant we were able to offer quality of service every time, and we also made sure we stayed on top of all the new styles and trends. In time we opened a school in St Christopher's Place, off Oxford Street, to train hairdressers using the knowledge we'd learned. We became quite influential for new techniques like plaiting and weaving, and our name started to spread all over the world. We travelled extensively putting on seminars and big exhibitions, where other hairdressers would come to see what we were doing.

In keeping with my childhood fascination with building, I was constantly looking for ways of expanding the business and building on our growing reputation. We branched out into doing videos and brought out a step-by-step book, the first of many. We've now done 26 books and they've been very successful. I remember we had the third book called *One Step Beyond* on sale at our Wembley show and we sold 5,000 in one hit. It was tremendous. Exciting new things were happening at that time and we were right in the heart of it.

By the late 1970s and early 1980s, we had the salons in Mayfair and Sloane Square and the school in St Christopher's Place, but we still wanted to expand, so we decided to start moving into products. By that time a big product company had offered us an opportunity to tour the US doing big shows. The TONI&GUY Artistic Team, headed by Bruno, went to every part of the US doing shows and seminars, but we soon discovered that some of the products were not up to the standard we needed to create the kind of styles we were doing. The plaits, for example, needed a much stronger gel than was currently available at that time, so we started producing our own gel and mousse. We were always innovating and experimenting.

But we were so impressed with the set-up in the US that we made the decision to create a base in America and I spent quite a lot of time there establishing salons with Bruno. We opened our first salons in Dallas – at Sherry Lane, followed by Galleria and then North Park – with Bruno at the head. Soon he met and married an American girl, bought a house there and was completely settled and in charge of the American operation. He later told me that he didn't feel English, and he hadn't felt Italian, but after just a few months, he felt American.

Bruno went on to open more salons in the US, very successfully. Then we decided to get more into the product line and move the base of operations there. Previously we'd been making the products in Denmark, but now we moved to America, making products unique to us. We couldn't call it TONI&GUY because Gillette had trademarked Toni and they stopped us doing it, so we called the product range Tigi.

While all that was going on I spent a lot of time abroad. I travelled to Japan, Hong Kong and Singapore, but spent most of the time in the US. That's when I first started thinking about the five-year plan to become a millionaire. This was the 1980s and everyone was talking about how to get rich and the five-year plan. The whole country, all its three hundred million people, were thinking of plans to make money. It seemed anyone could become a millionaire. It was such a different attitude to Britain at the time.

It was also in the US that I learned how to talk to banks about money and get the kind of investment that I needed. I also started thinking of expansion on a much bigger scale. The idea that kept coming back to me was franchising.

The thing I'd found with our salons in England was that we'd build up a fantastic team, almost like the Premiership, winning awards and getting a great reputation and becoming very successful. But ultimately there would come a point where there was nowhere for them to grow and expand further. So, naturally, some would move on, emigrate to other countries like Australia and the US, some would start their own business – often rival hairdressing salons – and some would give up hairdressing all together. So then we would then build up another team with the younger generation, then history would repeat itself.

That was when we decided that franchising the TONI&GUY brand was the way forward. Enabling them to set up their own salons, still under the umbrella of the main group and using the same training, products and ethos, meant there was some natural progression for all this talent, and we wouldn't end up losing it. It would allow them to stay in the company and it would allow the company to grow, which fitted right into my passion for building. It also allowed the younger generation to move up to the next level.

This way we could have many more salons, plus it would give us opportunities down the line for expanding our product range and using them in all the salons. We could also start more academies to train staff both nationwide and globally. The education, the books, the PR, the uniforms, the tools, the furniture – we had the whole structure. Since then we've moved on to other levels with our own TV channel, magazine and computer program. It was when I came back from America that I saw that opportunity, that potential, and that was the moment I started on course to make my first million.

It wasn't just me who was en route to becoming a millionaire. Franchising was also responsible for creating lots of other millionaires, who'd gone off to open their own successful salons under the TONI&GUY banner. As we started to open ten then 20 franchises in the late 1980s, that's when the money finally started coming in.

The plan at that stage was to open thousands of salons, but gradually more restrictions came into play, more Health and Safety and employment regulations. So I decided that it was better to stop at a few hundred salons and consolidate, then expand in different ways. The real proof that our strategy was going to work came with the recession of the early 1990s. Lots of businesses were failing, but we weathered that and that was a sign we were doing well. We provided the best service. We came out much stronger and much more disciplined. We hadn't been too extravagant, we'd consolidated our gains and we were working really well. By 1992 we knew we were on the right track.

Looking back, the key to our success was that we were always changing. The world changes, and in business it's essential that you change with it. If you don't change you'll fail. Look at the USSR. It was such a big, powerful country but they were so rigid in their rules, they wouldn't change one little thing. If they'd just allowed people to have a few fridges, a few cars, they might have survived but they wouldn't change because they were too afraid of capitalism to move a little. In business you have to remain flexible and keep a strong image of the bigger picture in your head at all times. That's how we created that first million and more from those franchises. After that a lot of franchisees also became millionaires, so we kept on growing.

The shift in spending power after that first recession also helped us to expand. In the UK, although you had 60million people, only a fraction of those at that time had spending power, so you could only open in London and a few other places. But after 1992/3, places like Manchester, Birmingham and Leeds developed to the same level as London, and then all the British towns developed to the point where a large proportion of people had the money to go to the salon. From dustman to office worker, they could all afford it, and that allowed us to grow.

The thing is that TONI&GUY aims to be the best salon in whichever area it's in. Of course, you can't always control every aspect of every salon and sometimes problems crop up. But we keep the risk of this to a minimum because everyone is trained by our academy and it takes five years to do the full course. We used to joke that it took the same length of time to train to become a dentist.

Since then we've gone from strength to strength, and the company has grown beyond even my wildest dreams. We've now got more than 400 salons worldwide, plus 28 academies, the product ranges, the Café Fratelli restaurant chain, TONI&GUY Opticians and the in-house TV channel. We've also got our own charity called the TONI&GUY Charitable Foundation, which raises money for sick and disadvantaged children. We are all very proud of this, and the money raised has built our very own

TONI&GUY children's ward in the Kings College Hospital in London, helping to save the lives of hundreds of sick children in the UK.

In 2003, we de-merged with the American branch. Now Guy, Bruno and Anthony run TONI&GUY in America and the Tigi brand, while my wife and I, our daughter Sacha and son Christian look after things in the UK and the rest of the globe. The press tried to create a story about sibling rivalry but that couldn't be further from the truth. After the de-merger I made a television programme and was interviewed by newspapers and magazines. It generated lots of PR, and everyone wanted to get the gossip and asked me why we had separated, why everything had gone bitterly wrong. Basically they were wanting to get some mud-slinging from me, so they were disappointed that there was no gossip or juicy story and that it was merely a business and financial decision.

We love each other and are one family, and there's no way anyone can anyone come between us. We had a great time building the company. We spent many, many years together. Of course I'm sad they're all in America but everyone has to go some time. It's like when your children leave. The de-merger was just about business. We're still a very close family.

It makes me so happy that my own children have now joined the business. Sacha is the global creative director of TONI&GUY, and is also responsible for TONI&GUY products and involved in our newest brand, label.m. We started it three years ago and now we're in 56 countries. Our ambition is to make label.m the biggest product company in the world! The whole process is very precise, to have the best packaging and be the best professional haircare line. The products are tested dozens of times by the TONI&GUY International Artistic Team until it is perfect and of the highest standard.

Christian is now in charge of our Essensuals brand and is growing the company and making it very strong. My other son, Pierre, is an actor and a director of Cipher Films, which produced movies such as *Kidulthood* in 2006 and *Adulthood* in 2008. He also produced a short film called *Nits*, which was nominated for a BAFTA in 2004. I am very proud of all of my children.

I count myself very lucky. I have a lovely family. I'm still in love with my wife, and I have a job I love. Every day I say thank God I've been given another day on this Earth, where I can support my family and grow my business, or go to Sloane Square and cut hair. I still go into the salon on a Saturday and cut hair for clients, some of whom I've known for 30 years. That's my idea of relaxation. I still love the whole process of cutting hair – I love chatting to the clients and trying out new styles and our new products, and I love being part of the team in the salon. I charge just the same as the other stylists. Why wouldn't I? I'm doing something I love, and I'm being paid for it! It's ridiculous!

Cutting hair is my hobby. I still have customers who remember my dad. Sometimes if a regular customer doesn't come, I call them up to make sure nothing has happened to them. I worry about them. It's like losing a child. I have one lady I hadn't seen for a while. I called her finally and she said, 'I'd love to come and see you but I've had chemotherapy and there's no hair for you to work with!' Only last week I saw her name in the appointment book and I was like a baby with candy – I was so excited! Her hair has grown back now and I gave her a great haircut.

People often say to me, 'What keeps you motivated to keep going now? You have all this money, your family is secure. Why don't you slow down?' But my motivation now is just the same as it was at the beginning – to keep expanding the company. I'll never stop building. I'd like to work towards leaving the company in good hands when the time comes. Sure, I see myself appearing in this or that Rich List or read I'm worth X amount of money but it doesn't mean anything to me. I feel that if you give me a nice plate of pasta and a good quality glass of wine and a colour TV so I can watch the football, I'll be OK. I don't need a Rolls-Royce. I don't need material things. You can have £10million or you can have £100million or you can have £200million. At the end of the day you just make a bigger bonfire, don't you?

What is important is your achievements. Two years ago I was awarded a *Cavaliere Ufficiale*, the Italian equivalent of a knighthood. Receiving this was quite amazing – being honoured by my home country even though I left it when I was 14. Then more recently I was awarded an Honorary

OBE by the Queen. This was something very, very special to me, as I have lived here almost all of my life, my family are here, my wife my children and grandchildren, my livelihood, so it was the ultimate honour. These recognitions mean more to me than any amount of money.

I'm not a big spender. When I fly to Italy with my wife we go club class but when I go on my own I go economy. I think it's foolish wasting money like that – I'd rather give it to charity. It's the same plane after all. I like to drive a nice car. I've got a BMW X5 with seven seats, so I only need one car instead of two when I go out with my family and friends. And we recently bought a house in Italy, in Sorrento. We'd been looking for 12 years and finally found a small villa. My wife has desperately wanted a home in Italy for a while now. Myself, I'd be happier staying in hotels.

Apart from that, what do I need money for? I get sick on yachts so it's not the thing for me. I don't particularly like fast cars and I don't like flying that much. But I like the security of having money. You know what would upset me more than anything? If one of my children or my family came to me and said, 'I need some help financially,' and I couldn't give it to them. Being able to help people gives me great joy. But in general, I'm economical. I don't like waste – I get upset when I see it.

I'm always being asked for advice for people starting out. All I'd say is if you've got love and affection around you and if you really believe in what you're doing, go out and do it 100 per cent. Don't do it ninety per cent or eighty per cent.

Go in and immerse yourself completely. Sometimes when I look back, I'm amazed at what we've achieved after arriving in this country with so little. I've had a great life, and I wouldn't have changed anything. But I'm not complacent. I would never be complacent – and there's still so much more to do.

A lot of people say to me, 'So now you have arrived!' as if I've reached some kind of finishing line. I say, 'So you think I'm just about dead?' In Italian, if you run a race, when you 'arrive', it means you're finished. And you know what? I'm only just beginning. Let's start another race.

Friends Again...

Tammy Cohen

From the moment the first social networking site putting old school friends in contact with one another appeared, the nation has been gripped by a frenzy of nostalgia as long-forgotten classmates and old flames spring once again to life through the click of a mouse.

Friends Again... is packed with incredible stories, including:

- The father reunited with his children after twenty-five years of searching.
- The childhood sweethearts who finally tied the knot more than a quarter of a century after drifting apart.
- The wife who discovered her husband was a bigamist by reading about his 'wedding' on his website profile.

The past is a Pandora's box of heightened emotions and seductive nostalgia. Once you open it up, it's very easy to get sucked inside. The consequences can be life changing.

ISBN 978-1-84454-638-1

John Blake Publishing

Coming Soon